THE QUEEN'S CLASSICS
CERTIFICATE BOOKS

*

ALDOUS HUXLEY
SELECTED ESSAYS

Aldous Huxley
SELECTED ESSAYS

Edited by
HAROLD RAYMOND, M.A.
With an Introduction by
FRANK WHITEHEAD, M.A.
Senior Lecturer in English and Education
University of Sheffield
Institute of Edncation

Chatto and Windus
LONDON

Published by
Chatto & Windus (Educational) Ltd
42 William IV Street
London w.c. 2

★

Clarke, Irwin & Co. Ltd
Toronto

*First published in Queen's Classics
Certificate Books 1961
Reprinted 1967*

Printed in Great Britain by
Lowe & Brydone (Printers) Ltd,
London

Contents

CONTENTS

Suggestions for further reading

Aldous Huxley's output is so voluminous that a comprehensive list of all his works would occupy several pages. The reader may wish to study his writings further and the following list, although not exhaustive, will provide an introduction to the many aspects of Huxley's work.

Fiction: Antic Hay; Point Counter Point; Eyeless in Gaza; Brave New World; Ape and Essence

Biography: Grey Eminence

Belles Lettres: Ends and Means; Brave New World Revisited; Texts and Pretexts; The Perennial Philosophy

The greater part of Huxley's essays, forty-eight in number, appear in a selection, approved by him, entitled *Collected Essays* (1960).

INTRODUCTION

MANY of us who grew up in the twenties and thirties still remember the heady excitement which accompanied our first acquaintance with the novels, essays and short stories of Aldous Huxley. We recall with gratitude a sense of liberation from widely-held but inert conventional assumptions; an awareness of new intellectual worlds opening out before us; and a new-found realization (no less important perhaps in the long run) that wit and moral responsibility need not be irreconcilable. In this Introduction the particular claim I wish to make for Huxley is that he is a highly educative writer. By this I mean that he can be read with exceptional profit by the intelligent young at the age when they are making up their minds about their fundamental tenets and goals—about the kind of person they want to be, the kind of beliefs they are able to hold, the kind of life they intend to lead. And I believe that this is no less true in the nineteen-sixties than it was twenty-five or thirty-five years ago. Indeed it is a demonstrable fact of experience that young people to-day, when they can be induced to read Huxley, find in him much that seems to them immediately relevant to the very issues which they care most deeply about; a striking testimony, surely, to the centrality of Huxley's concerns and the penetration of his social comment.

In part at least Huxley's power to educate is due to the extraordinary range and diversity of his interests. More than any other English writer of the present century he has striven to realize in his own person the ideal of the fully educated man—the 'all-rounder' who is at home in the culture of many different civilizations at many different periods, who is well informed about recent developments in the physical, biological and social sciences, as well as in philosophy and mathematics, and who at the same time is an alert and acute observer of all that goes on around him in the day-to-day business of human living. Even in the present limited selection from his writings there is impressive evidence of the extent to which he has succeeded in this aim. Literary criticism, painting, architecture, political democracy, economics, education, the social applications of science, over-population, advertisements, the celebration of Christmas—all these topics and many more are treated in this volume with a complete assurance that could come only from a uniquely well-furnished mind. We can readily believe him when he tells us in the early essay 'Books for the Journey' that at that time he never passed a day away from home without taking with him a volume of the *Encyclopaedia Britannica*—to be used, be it noted, 'only for amusement'. This remarkable spread of mental capacity in Huxley must no doubt owe a good deal to his heredity and family background; it is perhaps natural that in one who is the great-grandson of Dr Arnold of Rugby, the grandson of T. H. Huxley, the great-nephew of Matthew Arnold, and the brother of Sir Julian Huxley, we should detect no sign of that fatal split between the 'two cultures', literary and scientific, which Sir Charles Snow has lately warned us about. And certainly we can be confident that the arts student and the science student alike will gain from reading Huxley both a greatly increased breadth of mental reference, and a deepened understanding of the place which their own specialism occupies in the whole universe of human knowledge and experience.

At the same time it must be admitted that there is one important respect in which Huxley falls short in his ambition to be the complete twentieth-century man. Is there not after all a grain of truth concealed within Elizabeth Bowen's observation that Aldous Huxley is not only a very clever person but also 'the stupid person's idea of the clever person'? Granted that we do not need to read very far in his work to rid ourselves of any illusory picture of him as merely a frigid intellectual, a thinking-machine without a heart. Yet if we set him beside that very greatest of his contemporaries, D. H. Lawrence (who was also for many years one of his close personal friends), we do miss in Huxley a certain wholeness of natural emotional life; and we become aware, by contrast, of a limitation of spontaneous intuitive sympathy which makes us doubt if we should ever think of the term 'wisdom' in connection with Huxley, for all his 'cleverness'. Inevitably it is in his fiction that this defect matters most; and it may be suggested that we read, and shall continue to read, his novels for much the same reasons that we read his other prose writings—essentially, that is, as a deployment of ideas (fascinating, resourceful, truly educative) rather than as creative works of art.

To make this limiting judgment is not to dismiss Huxley's fiction as of little account. The earlier novels especially contain much that is wonderfully entertaining, while the later ones are often powerful and disturbing in a way which forces on the reader a valuable readjustment of settled habits of thinking and feeling. Nevertheless even in his two most ambitious works—*Point Counter Point* (1929) and *Eyeless in Gaza* (1936)—we seldom feel ourselves in the presence of that unforced creative vitality which is the distinguishing mark of the born novelist.

Huxley's awareness of his own deficiency in this respect seems to have contributed a good deal to the intense admiration which he felt and showed for D. H. Lawrence. Certainly his early and generous recognition of Lawrence's genius is very much to his credit in every way; and the essay with which he prefaced his collection of Lawrence's letters (an essay which is unfortunately too long to be included in this selection) is both a moving tribute to his friend and one of his finest and most maturely balanced pieces of literary criticism. We cannot of course tell how long Huxley would have continued to look to Lawrence's influence to supply that which he felt to be lacking in himself, nor how fruitful this influence might have proved. After Lawrence's death in 1930, however, Huxley increasingly turned for his remedy to the deliberate cultivation of those states of heightened consciousness which it is customary to call 'mystical'. This interest in the techniques of mystical contemplation is shown most explicitly in *The Perennial Philosophy* (1946), an anthology of mystical writings accompanied by Huxley's own commentary; but a similar preoccupation informs the important book *Ends and Means* (1937), in which an examination of the ethical basis of pacifism is intermingled with an extended exposition of the spiritual ideal of 'non-attachment'. This aspect of Huxley's thought is difficult and cannot be represented satisfactorily in brief extracts; so that (apart from the hints of his attitude which can be gleaned from the essay on El Greco) no attempt has been made to include it in the present selection. The reader needs to realize, however, that in his later writings Huxley has moved a long way from the standpoint expressed in his remark (in the early essay 'Cawnpore') that: 'The Other World—the world of metaphysics and religion—can never possibly be as interesting as this world . . .'

Huxley's fiction, then, is well worth reading, yet one's recommendation of it needs to be tempered with a certain qualifying caution. The novels have a salutary moral seriousness, but it seems to me that their sense of the positive values of human living is not firm enough to counter-balance the 'desperate courage of repulsion and repudiation' which Lawrence noted in them. (The unqualified success of *Brave New World*, a satirical Utopia as unforgettable in its own way as those created by Swift in *Gulliver's Travels*, perhaps confirms one's impression that it is the negative and destructive impulses which are able most fully to unleash the writer's creative energy.) In the case of the essays no such caution is necessary. Here we can salute unreservedly Huxley's potency as an educative influence—a potency which we see as deriving in the first place from the truly remarkable sweep and comprehensiveness of his mental activity. Does this account seem to suggest that Huxley is essentially a great popularizer of other people's ideas? There is no need to shy away from the term. In our present age of intellectual specialization, when the inescapable tendency of all higher education is to lead each one of us to know progressively more and more about less and less, there is a crying need for communications to be kept open between the different branches of knowledge. True popularization is a vital and honourable function; and it is also an immensely difficult one, since it calls for a presentation of new concepts which makes them intelligible to the non-expert reader while at the same time doing full justice to their complexity. In reality, however, Huxley is more than merely an outstandingly lucid middleman of ideas, for his wide reading has always been accompanied by exceptional powers of discrimination. Whatever the topic he seems able unerringly to select the significant from the trivial, and to organize the material so gathered into a pattern of thinking which relates it, in a direct and fully responsible way, to the key-problem of how to live, in our twentieth-century world, a life which is fully human.

Moreover these patterns of thinking have a quality which we recognize as peculiarly valuable to the educative process. Persuasive though his arguments often are, he seems to be calling on us not so much to accept them as to think for ourselves. The movement of the prose itself has an agility which affects us as a challenge and stimulus to similar independent mental activity on our own part. We note too the unfailing persistence with which Huxley questions our most cherished assumptions. Do we really believe that increased leisure will enable us to lead fuller and happier lives? What grounds have we, in the observed facts of experience, for our complacent faith that political democracy is the best form of government? How much reality is there to our conventional notions of progress when, in the self-proclaimed age of inventions, 'nobody has succeeded in inventing a new pleasure'? The challenge, it will be observed, is not only to our intellectual assumptions, but also to the values by which we live. Notice particularly, in the present volume, how radically Huxley compels us to reassess the values which are proclaimed every day by the organs of Admass, and how searching is his criticism of the vulgarity which lies at the heart of our commercial civilization.

At times this deliberate provocativeness takes the form of paradox. 'Time, as we know it, is a very recent invention.' Thus runs the opening sentence of the essay 'Time and the Machine'; and having let our eyes fall on it, can we fail to be stirred into reading on, in a spirit either curious or contentious, to see how he can justify this challenging proposition? Perhaps on occasion, particularly in the earlier essays, formulations of this kind seem to arise mainly from a clever young man's delight in shocking his audience. More commonly, however, paradox in Huxley is neither an arbitrary topsy-turviness nor a superficial play with words, but expresses an alert perception of unlikely relationships which no one else would ever have noticed. Consider, for instance, the opening of his argument on 'Comfort':

> What have comfort and cleanliness to do with politics, morals, and religion? At a first glance one would say that there was and could be no causal connection between armchairs and democracies, sofas and the relaxation of the family system, hot baths and the decay of Christian orthodoxy. But look more closely. . . .

And sure enough, Huxley goes on to convince us that such a connection can indeed be established and is no mere flight of fancy. Wit in Huxley, it will be observed, is integral to the whole structure of his thought and sensibility; it is never merely applied to the surface like stucco on a wall. And the same could be said of the other qualities we find to admire in his prose—the vivid energy, the clarity and precision, the ease with which he wears his erudition.

One further merit of Huxley's writings deserves to be stressed. He has shown himself remarkably far-sighted in his social analysis—able to recognize and diagnose conditions and trends of whose importance few others had, at the time, the least inkling. One need refer only to the prescience of his remarks about the use of leisure in the future (so apt in their application to the present day that it is hard to believe they first appeared as long ago as 1925), or to the way in which the *Brave New World* he depicted with such frightening persuasiveness in 1931 seems, in 1960, even more nightmarishly possible, rather than less. And can there be much doubt that the two most recent essays in the present volume (on 'Over-population' and on 'The Arts of Selling') are likely to wear equally well?

This far-sightedness has a bearing on one other question

which needs to be discussed here. These essays have been written over a period of more than thirty-five years; moreover these years have been ones during which the world has changed far more rapidly than ever before in the history of mankind. Inevitably therefore some of the earlier pieces have dated in certain respects. There is no reason why this need confuse or disturb the present-day reader, so long as he takes the trouble to notice the date when the essay was first published. Thus the sixth-former of to-day when reading the essay on 'Education' (1927) will note mentally that classes nowadays are not usually *quite* so large as all that, that promotion from one form to the next is now usually by age rather than by attainment, that the methods of education which Huxley commends as 'psychologically sound' can now be found operating not only in infant schools, but also in some junior schools; and so on. But the real point is that, although some of Huxley's detailed instances are no longer applicable, his central thesis is still amazingly relevant. The 'two enormous fallacies' which he exposed so trenchantly may have taken some hard knocks in the intervening thirty years, but they are still very much alive. In a similar way in 'Miahuatlan' it is merely the terms of Huxley's argument which have dated. His comparison between the industrial civilization of the United States and the pre-industrial way of life of the Mexican Indians belongs to 1934; but the problem this comparison helps to illuminate (the problem of 'reconciling the primitive with the civilized', of how to contrive 'the wedding of primitive with civilized virtues') is still with us. And again while there are certain details in 'Revolutions' (about relative earnings in different occupations, for instance) which the young reader should be warned to accept with caution, I do not think there is much danger of anyone being misled by them, so long as some sense of historical perspective can be maintained.

In general what I have claimed for Huxley as an essayist is that he enlarges our mental horizons and stimulates us to do our own thinking. It is surely true also that he refuses to be kept at a distance and cannot easily be relegated to the category of those who merely interest or amuse us without ever really affecting our lives. Whether or not we agree with what he has to say, we find ourselves recognizing that the issues he raises are ones that matter, and that the results of our thinking about them need to be applied to ourselves and incorporated in our own way of living. It is thus that some readers of this volume will no doubt take to themselves, in an immediate and personal way, his comments on 'the tendency, so much encouraged by the examination system, to mug up other people's judgments and repeat them mechanically and without reflection'. And in their very nature Huxley's writings are, thank goodness, as formidable an enemy to this tendency as one could possibly wish for.

FRANK WHITEHEAD

SIR CHRISTOPHER WREN

From *On the Margin* (1923)

THAT an Englishman should be a very great plastic artist is always rather surprising. Perhaps it is a matter of mere chance; perhaps it has something to do with our national character—if such a thing really exists. But, whatever may be the cause, the fact remains that England has produced very few artists of first-class importance. The Renaissance, as it spread, like some marvellous infectious disease of the spirit, across the face of Europe, manifested itself in different countries by different symptoms. In Italy, the country of its origin, the Renaissance was, more than anything, an outburst of painting, architecture and sculpture. Scholarship and religious reformation were, in Germany, the typical manifestations of the disease. But when this gorgeous spiritual measles crossed the English Channel, its symptoms were almost exclusively literary. The first premonitory touch of the infection from Italy 'brought out' Chaucer. With the next bout of the disease England produced the Elizabethans. But among all these poets there was not a single plastic artist whose name we so much as remember.

And then, suddenly, the seventeenth century gave birth to two English artists of genius. It produced Inigo Jones and, a little later, Wren. Wren died, at the age of more than ninety, in the spring of 1723. We are celebrating to-day his bi-centenary —celebrating it not merely by antiquarian talk and scholarly appreciations of his style but also (the signs are not wanting) in a more concrete and living way: by taking a renewed interest in the art of which he was so great a master and by reverting in our practice to that fine tradition which he, with his predecessor, Inigo, inaugurated.

An anniversary celebration is an act of what Wordsworth would have called 'natural piety'; an act by which past is linked with present and of the vague, interminable series of the days a single comprehensible and logical unity is created in our minds. At the coming of the centenaries we like to remember the great men of the past, not so much by way of historical exercise, but that we may see precisely where, in relation to their achievement, we stand at the present time, that we may appraise the life still left in their spirit and apply to ourselves the moral of their example. I have no intention in this article of giving a biography of Wren, a list of his works, or a technical account of his style and methods. I propose to do no more than describe, in the most general terms, the nature of his achievement and its significance to ourselves.

Wren was a good architect. But since it is important to know precisely what we are talking about, let us begin by asking ourselves what good architecture is. Descending with majesty from his private Sinai, Mr Ruskin dictated to a whole generation of Englishmen the aesthetic Law. On monolithic tables that were the Stones of Venice he wrote the great truths that had been revealed to him. Here is one of them:

> It is to be generally observed that the proportions of buildings have nothing to do with the style or general merit of their architecture. An architect trained in the worst schools and utterly devoid of all meaning or purpose in his work, may yet have such a natural gift of massing and grouping as will render his structure effective when seen at a distance.

Now it is to be generally observed, as he himself would say, that in all matters connected with art, Ruskin is to be interpreted as we interpret dreams—that is to say, as signifying precisely the opposite of what he says. Thus, when we find him saying that good architecture has nothing to do with proportion or the judicious disposition of masses and that the general effect counts for nothing at all, we may take it as more or less definitely proven that good architecture is, in fact, almost entirely a matter of proportion and massing, and that the general effect of the whole work counts for nearly everything. Interpreted according to this simple oneirocritical method, Ruskin's pontifical pronouncement may be taken as explaining briefly and clearly the secrets of good architecture. That is why I have chosen this quotation to be the text of my discourse on Wren.

For the qualities which most obviously distinguish Wren's work are precisely those which Ruskin so contemptuously disparages and which we, by our process of interpretation, have singled out as the essentially architectural qualities. In all that Wren designed—I am speaking of the works of his maturity; for at the beginning of his career he was still an unpractised amateur, and at the end, though still on occasion wonderfully successful, a very old man—we see a faultless proportion, a felicitous massing and contrasting of forms. He conceived his buildings as three-dimensional designs which should be seen, from every point of view, as harmoniously proportioned wholes. (With regard to the exteriors this, of course, is true only of those buildings which *can* be seen from all sides. Like all true architects, Wren preferred to build in positions where his work could be appreciated three-dimensionally. But he was also a wonderful maker of façades; witness his Middle Temple gateway and his houses in King's Bench Walk.) He possessed in the highest degree that instinctive sense of proportion and scale which enabled him to embody his conception in brick and stone. In his great masterpiece of St Paul's every part of the building, seen from within or without, seems to stand in a certain satisfying and harmonious relation to every other part. The same is true even of the smallest works belonging to the period of Wren's maturity. On its smaller scale and different plane, such a building as Rochester Guildhall is as beautiful, because as harmonious in the relation of all its parts, as St Paul's.

Of Wren's other purely architectural qualities I shall speak but briefly. He was, to begin with, an engineer of inexhaustible resource; one who could always be relied upon to find the best possible solution to any problem, from blowing up the ruins of old St Paul's to providing the new with a dome that should be at once beautiful and thoroughly safe. As a designer he exhibited the same practical ingenuity. No architect has known how to make so much of a difficult site and cheap materials. The man who built the City churches was a practical genius of no common order. He was also an artist of profoundly original mind. This originality reveals itself in the way in which he combines the accepted features of classical Renaissance architecture into new designs that were entirely English and his own. The steeples of his City churches provide us with an obvious example of this originality. His domestic architecture—that wonderful application of classical principles to the best in the native tradition—is another.

But Wren's most characteristic quality—the quality which gives to his work, over and above its pure beauty, its own peculiar character and charm—is a quality rather moral than aesthetic. Of Chelsea Hospital, Carlyle once remarked that it was 'obviously the work of a gentleman'. The words are illuminating. Everything that Wren did was the work of a gentleman; that is the secret of its peculiar character. For Wren was a great gentleman: one who valued dignity and restraint and who, respecting himself, respected also humanity; one who desired that men and women should live with the dignity, even the grandeur, befitting their proud human title; one who despised meanness and oddity as much as vulgar ostentation; one who admired reason and order, who distrusted all extravagance and excess. A gentleman, the finished product of an old and ordered civilization.

Wren, the restrained and dignified gentleman, stands out most clearly when we compare him with his Italian contemporaries. The baroque artists of the seventeenth century were interested above everything in the new, the startling, the astonishing; they strained after impossible grandeurs, unheard-of violences. The architectural ideals of which they dreamed were more suitable for embodiment in theatrical cardboard than in stone. And indeed, the late seventeenth and early eighteenth century was the golden age of scene-painting in Italy. The artists who painted the settings for the elder Scarlatti's operas, the later Bibienas and Piranesis, came nearer to reaching the wild Italian ideal than ever mere architects like Borromini or

Bernini, their imaginations cramped by the stubbornness of stone and the unsleeping activities of gravitations, could hope to do.

How vastly different is the baroque theatricality from Wren's sober restraint! Wren was a master of the grand style; but he never dreamed of building for effect alone. He was never theatrical or showy, never pretentious or vulgar. St Paul's is a monument of temperance and chastity. His great palace at Hampton Court is no gaudy stage-setting for the farce of absolute monarchy. It is a country gentleman's house—more spacious, of course, and with statelier rooms and more impressive vistas—but still a house meant to be lived in by someone who was a man as well as a king. But if his palaces might have housed, without the least incongruity, a well-bred gentleman, conversely his common houses were always dignified enough, however small, to be places in miniature and the homes of kings.

In the course of two hundred years which have elapsed since his death, Wren's successors have often departed, with melancholy results, from the tradition of which he was the founder. They have forgotten, in their architecture, the art of being gentlemen. Infected by a touch of the baroque *folie de grandeur*, the architects of the eighteenth century built houses in imitation of Versailles and Caserta—huge stage houses, all for show and magnificence and all but impossible to live in.

The architects of the nineteenth century sinned in a diametrically opposite way—towards meanness and a negation of art. Senselessly preoccupied with details, they created the nightmare architecture of 'features'. The sham Gothic of early Victorian times yielded at the end of the century to the nauseous affectation of 'sham-peasantry'. Big houses were built with all the irregularity and more than the 'quaintness' of cottages; suburban villas took the form of machine-made imitations of the Tudor peasant's hut. To all intents and purposes architecture ceased to exist; Ruskin had triumphed.

To-day, however, there are signs that architecture is coming back to that sane and dignified tradition of which Wren was the great exponent. Architects are building houses for gentlemen to live in. Let us hope that they will continue to do so. There may be sublimer types of men than the gentleman: there are saints, for example, and the great enthusiasts whose thoughts and actions move the world. But for practical purposes and in a civilized, orderly society, the gentleman remains, after all, the ideal man. The most profound religious emotions have been expressed in Gothic architecture. Human ambitions and aspirations have been most colossally reflected by the Romans and the Italians of the baroque. But it is in England that the golden mean of reasonableness and decency—the practical philosophy of the civilized man—has received its most elegant and dignified expression. The old gentleman who died two hundred years ago preached on the subject of civilization a number of sermons in stone. St Paul's and Greenwich, Trinity Library and Hampton Court, Chelsea, Kilmainham, Blackheath and Rochester, St Stephen's Wallbrook and St Mary Abchurch, Kensington orangery and Middle Temple gateway—these are the titles of a few of them. They have much, if we will but study them, to teach us.

VIEWS OF HOLLAND

From *Along the Road* (1925)

I HAVE always been rather partial to plane geometry; probably because it was the only branch of mathematics that was ever taught me in such a way that I could understand it. For though I have no belief in the power of education to turn public school boys into Newtons (it being quite obvious that, whatever opportunity may be offered, it is only those rare beings desirous of learning and possessing a certain amount of native ability who ever do learn anything), yet I must insist, in my own defence, that the system of mathematical instruction of which, at Eton, I was the unfortunate victim, was calculated not merely to turn my desire to learn into stubborn passive resistance, but also to stifle whatever rudimentary aptitude in this direction I might have possessed. But let that pass. Suffice to say that, in spite of my education and my congenital ineptitude, plane geometry has always charmed me by its simplicity and elegance, its elimination of detail and the individual case, its insistence on generalities.

My love for plane geometry prepared me to feel a special affection for Holland. For the Dutch landscape has all the qualities that make geometry so delightful. A tour in Holland is a tour through the first books of Euclid. Over a country that is the ideal plane surface of the geometry books, the roads and the canals trace out the shortest distances between point and point. In the interminable polders, the road-topped dykes and gleaming ditches intersect one another at right angles, a criss-cross of perfect parallels. Each rectangle of juicy meadowland contained between the intersecting dykes has identically the same area. Five kilometres long, three deep—the figures record themselves on the clock face of the cyclometer. Five by three by—how many? The demon of calculation possesses the mind. Rolling along those smooth brick roads between the canals, one strains one's eyes to count the dykes at right angles and parallel to one's own. One calculates the area of the polders they enclose. So many square kilometres. But the square kilometres have to be turned into acres. It is a fearful sum to do in one's head; the more so as one has forgotten how many square yards there are in an acre.

And all the time, as one advances the huge geometrical landscape spreads out on either side of the car like an opening fan. Along the level sky-line a score of windmills wave their arms like dancers in a geometrical ballet. Ineluctably, the laws of perspective lead away the long roads and shining waters to a misty vanishing point. Here and there—mere real irrelevancies in the midst of this ideal plain—a few black and white cows out of a picture by Cuyp browse indefatigably in the lush green grass or, remembering Paul Potter, mirror themselves like so many ruminating Narcissi, in the waters of a canal. Sometimes one passes a few human beings, deplorably out of place, but doing their best, generally, to make up for their ungeometrical appearance by mounting bicycles. The circular wheels suggest a variety of new theorems and a new task for the demon of calculation. Suppose the radius of the wheels to be fifteen inches; then fifteen times fifteen times *pi* will be the area. The only trouble is that one has forgotten the value of *pi*.

Hastily I exorcise the demon of calculation that I may be free to admire the farm-house on the opposite bank of the canal on our right. How perfectly it fits into the geometrical scheme! On a cube, cut down to about a third of its height, is placed a tall pyramid. That is the house. A plantation of trees, set in quincunx formation, surrounds it; the limits of its rectangular garden are drawn in water on the green plain, and beyond these neat ditches extend the interminable flat fields. There are no outhouses, no barns, no farm-yard with untidy stacks. The hay is stored under the huge pyramidal roof, and in the truncated cube below live, on one side the farmer and his family, on the other side (during winter only; for during the rest of the year they sleep in the fields) his black and white Cuyp cows. Every farmhouse in North Holland conforms to this type, which is traditional, and so perfectly fitted to the landscape that it would have been impossible to devise anything more suitable. An English farm with its ranges of straggling buildings, its unidy yard, full of animals, its haystacks and pigeon-cotes would be horribly out of place here. In the English landscape, which is all accidents, variety, detail and particular cases, it is perfect. But here, in this generalized and Euclidean North Holland, it would be a blot and a discord. Geometry calls for geometry; with a sense of the aesthetic proprieties which one cannot too highly admire, the Dutch had responded to the appeal of the landscape and have dotted the plane surface of their country with cubes and pyramids.

Delightful landscape! I know of no country that is more mentally exhilarating to travel in. No wonder Descartes preferred the Dutch to any other scene. It is the rationalist's paradise. One feels as one flies along in the teeth of one's own forty-mile-an-hour wind like a Cartesian Encyclopaedist—flushed with mental intoxication, convinced that Euclid is absolute reality, that God is a mathematician, that the universe is a simple affair that can be explained in terms of physics and mechanics, that all men are equally endowed with reason and that it is only a question of putting the right arguments before them to make them see the error of their ways and to inaugurate the reign of justice and common sense. Those were noble and touching dreams, commendable inebriations! We are soberer now. We have learnt that nothing is simple and rational except what we ourselves have invented; that God thinks neither in terms of Euclid nor of Riemann; that science has 'explained' nothing; that the more we know the more fantastic the world becomes and the profounder the surrounding darkness; that reason is unequally distributed; that instinct is the sole source of action; that prejudice is incomparably stronger than argument and that even in the twentieth century men behave as they did in the caves of Altamira and in the lake dwellings of Glastonbury. And symbolically one makes the same discoveries in Holland. For the polders are not unending, nor all the canals straight, not every house a wedded cube and pyramid, nor even the fundamental plane surface invariably plane. That delightful 'Last Ride Together' feeling that fills one, as one rolls along the brick-topped dykes between the canals is deceptive. The present is not eternal; the 'Last Ride' through plane geometry comes to a sudden end—in a town, in forests, in the sea coast, in a winding river or great estuary. It matters little which; all are fundamentally ungeometrical; each has power to dissipate in an instant all those 'paralogisms of rationalism' (as Professor Rougier calls them) which we have so fondly cherished among the polders. The towns have crooked streets thronged with people; the houses are of all shapes and sizes. The coast-line is not straight nor regularly curved and its dunes or its dykes (for it must be defended against the besieging waves by art if not by nature) rear themselves inexcusably out of the plane surface. The woods are unscientific in their shady mysteriousness and one cannot see them for all their individual trees. The rivers are tortuous and alive with boats and barges. The inlets of the sea are entirely shapeless. It is the real world again after the ideal—hopelessly diversified, complex and obscure; but, when the first regrets are over, equally charming with the geometrical landscape we have left behind. We shall find it more charming, indeed, if our minds are practical and extroverted. Personally, I balance my affections. For I love the inner world as much as the outer. When the outer vexes me, I retire to the rational simplicities of the inner—to the polders of the spirit. And when, in their turn, the polders seem unduly flat, the roads too straight and the laws of perspective too tyrannous, I emerge again into the pleasing confusion of untempered reality.

And how beautiful, how curious in Holland that confusion is! I think of Rotterdam with its enormous river and its great bridges, so crowded with the traffic of a metropolis that one has to wait in files, half a mile long, for one's turn to cross. I think of The Hague and how it tries to be elegant and only succeeds in being respectable and upper middle class; of Delft, the commercial city of three hundred years ago; of Haarlem where, in autumn, you see them carting bulbs as in other countries they

cart potatoes; of Hoorn on the Zuyder Zee, with its little har-
bour and seaward-looking castle, its absurd museum filled with
rich mixed rubbish, its huge storehouse of cheeses, like an old-
fashioned arsenal, where the workmen are busy all day long
polishing the yellow cannon balls on a kind of lathe and painting
them bright pink with an aniline stain. I think of Volendam—
one line of wooden houses perched on the sea wall, and another
line crouching in the low green fields behind the dyke. The
people at Volendam are dressed as for a musical comedy—*Miss
Hook of Holland*—the men in baggy trousers and short jackets,
the women in winged white caps, tight bodices, and fifteen superimposed petticoats. Five thousand tourists come daily to look at
them; but they still, by some miracle, retain their independence
and self-respect. I think of Amsterdam; the old town, like a
livelier Bruges, mirrors its high brick houses in the canals. In one
quarter an enormous courtesan sits smiling at every window, the
meatiest specimens of humanity I ever saw. At nine in the
morning, at lunch-time, at six in the afternoon, the streets are
suddenly filled with three hundred thousand bicycles; every one,
in Amsterdam, goes to and from his business on a pair of wheels.
For the pedestrian as well as for the motorist, it is a nightmare.
And they are all trick cyclists. Children of four carry children
of three on their handle-bars. Mothers pedal gaily along with
month-old infants sleeping in cradles fastened to the back carrier.
Messenger boys think nothing of taking two cubic metres of
parcels. Dairymen do their rounds on bicycles specially con-
structed to accommodate two hundred quart bottles of milk in
a tray between the two wheels. I have seen nursery gardeners
carrying four palms and a dozen of potted chrysanthemums on
their handle-bars. I have seen five people rising through the
traffic on one machine. The most daring feats of the circus and
the music hall are part of the quotidian routine in Amsterdam.

I think of the dunes near Schoorl. Seen from a little distance
across the plain they look like a range of enormous mountains
against the sky. Following with the eye that jagged silhouette
one can feel all the emotions aroused, shall we say, by the

spectacle of the Alps seen from Turin. The dunes are grand; one could write a canto from *Childe Harold* about them. And then, unfortunately, one realizes what for a moment one had forgotten, that this line of formidable peaks is not looking down at one from fifty miles away, over the curving flank of the planet; it is just a furlong distant, and the chimneys of the houses at its base reach nearly two-thirds of the way to the top. But what does that matter? With a little good will, I insist, one can feel in Holland all the emotions appropriate to Switzerland.

Yes, they are grand, the dunes of Schoorl and Groet. But I think the grandest sight I saw in non-geometrical Holland was Zaandam—Zaandam from a distance, across the plain.

We had been driving through the polders and the open country of North Holland. Zaandam was the first piece of ungeometrical reality since Alkmaer. Technically, Zaandam is not picturesque; the guide-book has little to say about it. It is a port and manufacturing town on the Zaan, a few miles north of Amsterdam; that is all. They make cocoa there and soap. The air at Zaandam is charged in alternative strata with delicious vapours of molten chocolate and the stench of boiling fat. In wharves by the shores of the river they store American grain and timber from the Baltic. It was the granaries that first announced, from a distance, the presence of Zaandam. Like the cathedrals of a new religion, yet unpreached, they towered up into the hazy autumn air— huge oblongs of concrete set on end, almost windowless, smooth and blankly grey. It was as though their whole force were directed vertically upwards; to look from windows horizontally across the world would have been a distraction; eyes were sacrificed to this upward purpose. And the direction of that purpose was emphasized by the lines of the alternately raised and lowered panels into which the wall spaces of the great buildings were divided—long fine lines of shadow running up unbrokenly through a hundred feet from base to summit. The builders of the papal palace at Avignon used a very similar device to give their castle its appearance of enormous height and formidable impendence. The raised panel and the shallow blind arches, impossibly long in the leg, with which they variegated the surface of the wall, impart to the whole building an impetuous upward tendency. It is the same with the grain elevators at Zaandam. In the haze of autumnal Holland I remembered Provence. And I remembered, as I watched those towering shapes growing larger and larger as we approached, Chartres and Bourges and Reims: gigantic silhouettes seen at the end of a day's driving, towards evening, against a pale sky, with the little lights of a city about their base.

But if at a distance, Zaandam, by its commercial monuments, reminds one of Provençal castles and the Gothic cathedrals of France, a nearer view proclaims it to be unequivocally Dutch. At the foot of the elevators and the only less enormous factories, in the atmosphere of chocolate and soap, lies the straggling town. The suburbs are long, but narrow; for they cling precariously to a knife-edge of land between two waters. The houses are small, made of wood and gaudily painted; with gardens as large as table-cloths, beautifully kept and filled—at any rate at the season when I saw them—with plushy begonias. In one, as large, in this case, as two table-cloths, were no less than fourteen large groups of statuary. In the streets are men in wooden shoes, smoking. Dogs drawing carts with brass pots in them. Innumerable bicycles. It is the real and not the ideal geometrical Holland, crowded, confusing, various, odd, charming. . . . But I sighed as we entered the town. The 'Last Ride Together' was over; the dear paralogisms of rationalism were left behind. It was now necessary to face the actual world of men—and to face it, in my case, with precisely five words of Dutch (and patois at that) learned years before for the benefit of a Flemish servant: 'Have you fed the cat?' No wonder I regretted the polders.

WORK AND LEISURE

From *Along the Road* (1925)

REFORMERS look forward to a time when efficient social organization and perfected machinery will do away with the necessity for severe and prolonged labour, making possible for all men and women an amount of leisure such as is enjoyed at the present day only by a privileged few. Nobody, in that golden age, will need to work more than four or five hours a day. The rest of every man's time will be his own, to do with whatsoever he likes.

It is difficult for any sensitive person not to sympathize with these aspirations. One must be most arrogantly certain of one's own super-manhood before one can complacently accept the slavery on which the possibility of being a superman is based. Poor Nietzsche ended by signing his letter 'Nietzsche Caesar' and died in a madhouse. Perhaps that is the price that must be paid—at any rate by the intelligent; for the placidly stupid never pay, just as they never receive, anything—for an unfaltering conviction of superiority.

But sympathy with an ideal need not make the sympathizer uncritical of it; one may feel strongly, but one must not therefore cease to think. The majority of human beings are oppressed by excessive labour of the most senseless kind. That fact may, and indeed should, arouse our indignation and our pity. But these emotions must not prevent us from criticizing the project of those who wish to change the present state of things. The social reformers desire to see a dispensation under which all men will have as much, or nearly as much leisure as is enjoyed by the leisured classes today. We may be permitted to doubt, for all our sympathy, whether the consummation is really, after all, so much to be desired.

Let us begin by asking one simple question: What is it proposed that human beings shall do with the leisure which social reorganization and perfected machinery are to give them?

Prophets of the future give fundamentally the same answer to this question, with slight variations according to their different tastes. Henri Poincaré, for example, imagined that the human beings of the future would fill their long leisures by 'contemplating the laws of nature'. Mr Bernard Shaw is of much the same opinion. Having ceased, by the time they are four years old, to take any interest in such childish things as love, art and the society of their fellow beings, the Ancients in *Back to Methuselah* devote their indefinitely prolonged existences to meditating on the mysterious and miraculous beauty of the cosmos. Mr H. G. Wells portrays in *Men like Gods* a race of athletic chemists and mathematical physicists who go about naked and, unlike Mr Shaw's austerer Ancients, make free love in a rational manner between the experiments. They also take an interest in the arts and are not above playing games.

These three answers to our question are typical. Different prophets may differ in their estimate of the relative importance of the various activities which make up what is generally known as 'the higher life'; but all agree that the lives of our leisured posterity will be high. They will eagerly make themselves acquainted with 'the best that has been thought or said' about everything; they will listen to concerts of the classiest music; they will practise the arts and handicrafts (at any rate until the time comes when even these occupations seem childish); they will study the sciences, philosophy, mathematics, and meditate on the lovely mystery of the world in which they live.

In a word, these leisured masses of a future which there is no reason to believe enormously remote—indeed, our grandchildren may live to see the establishment of the four-hour day—will do all the things which our leisured classes of the present time so conspicuously fail to do.

How many rich and leisured people are there now living, who spend their time contemplating the laws of nature? I cannot say; all I know is that I rarely meet them. Many of the leisured, it is true, devote themselves to the patronage and even the amateur practice of the arts. But any one who has moved among rich 'artistic' people knows how much of this cultivation of the arts is due to snobbery, how shallow and insincere their loudly voiced enthusiasms mostly are. The leisured classes take up art for the same reasons as they take up bridge—to escape from boredom. With sport and love-making, art helps to fill up the vacuum of their existence.

At Monte Carlo and Nice one meets the rich whose dominant interests are play and love. Two millions, according to my guide-book, annually visit Monte Carlo alone. Seven-eighths of the whole leisured population of Europe must concentrate themselves yearly on that strip of the coast. Five thousand jazz bands play daily for their delectation. A hundred thousand motor vehicles transport them from one place to another at great speed. Huge joint-stock companies offer them every kind of distraction, from roulette to golf. Legions of prostitutes assemble from all parts of the globe and enthusiastic amateurs of the gentle passion abound. For four months in the year the French Riviera is an earthly paradise. When the four months are over, the leisured rich return to their northerly homes, where they find awaiting them less splendid, but quite authentic *succursales* of the paradise they have left behind.

The leisured rich at Monte Carlo are those, I have said, whose chief resources against ennui or serious thoughts are love and play. Many of them are also 'artistic'. But it is not, I think, at Monte Carlo that the best specimens of the artistic rich are to be found. To see them at their best one must go to Florence. Florence is the home of those who cultivate with an equal ardour Mah-jongg and a passion for Fra Angelico. Over tea and crumpets they talk, if they are too old for love themselves, of their lascivious juniors; but they also make sketches in water colour and read the *Little Flowers of St Francis*.

I must not, in justice to the leisured rich, omit to mention that respectable minority of them who occupy themselves with works of charity (not to mention tyranny), with politics, with local administration and occasionally with scholarly or scientific studies. I hesitate to use the word 'service'; for it has been held up so frequently as an ideal and by such a riff-raff of newspaper proprietors, hard-headed business men and professional moralists from the Y.M.C.A., that it has lost all real significance. The 'ideal of service' is achieved, according to our modern messiahs, by those who do efficient and profitable business with just enough honesty to keep them out of gaol. Plain shopkeeping is thus exalted into a beautiful virtue. The ideal of service which animates the best part of the English leisured class has nothing to do with the ideals of service so frequently mentioned by advertisers in American magazines. If I had not made this clear, my praise might have been thought, if not positively insulting, at least most damnably faint.

There exists, then, an admirable minority. But even when the minority and its occupations are duly taken into account, it cannot honestly be said that the leisured classes of the present time, or indeed of any historical period of which we have knowledge, provide a very good advertisement for leisure. The contemplation of richly leisured life in Monte Carlo and even in artistic Florence is by no means cheering or elevating.

Nor are we much reassured when we consider the occupations of the unleisured poor during those brief hours of repose allowed them between their work and their sleep. Watching other people play games, looking at cinema films, reading newspapers and indifferent fiction, listening to radio concerts and gramophone records and going from place to place in trains and omnibuses—these, I suppose, are the principal occupations of the working-man's leisure. Their cheapness is all that distinguishes them from the diversions of the rich. Prolong the leisure and what will happen? There will have to be more cinemas, more newspapers, more bad fiction, more radios and more cheap automobiles. If wealth and education increase with the leisure, than there will have to be more Russian Ballets as well as more movies, more *Timeses* as well as more *Daily Mails*, more casinos as well as more bookies and football matches, more expensive operas as well as more gramophone records, more Hugh Walpoles as well as more Nat Goulds. Acting on the same organisms the same causes may be expected to produce the same effects. And for all ordinary purposes, and so far as historical time is concerned, human nature is practically unchanging; the organism does remain the same. *Argal*, as Launcelot Gobbo would have said. . . .

This being so, we must further assume that increase of leisure will be accompanied by a correspondingly increased incidence of those spiritual maladies—ennui, restlessness, spleen and general world-weariness—which afflict and have always afflicted the leisured classes now and in the past.

Another result of increased leisure, provided that it is accompanied by a tolerably high standard of living, will be a very much increased interest on the part of what is now the working class in all matters of an amorous nature. Love, in all its complicated luxuriance, can only flourish in a society composed of well-fed, unemployed people. Examine the literature which has been written by and for members of the leisured classes and compare it with popular working-class literature. Compare *La Princesse de Clèves* with *The Pilgrim's Progress*, Proust with Charles Garvice, Chaucer's *Troilus and Cressida* with the ballads. It becomes at once sufficiently evident that the leisured classes do take and have always taken a much keener and, I might say, more professional interest in love than the workers. A man cannot work hard and at the same time conduct elaborate love affairs. Making love, at any rate in the style in which unemployed women desire it to be made, is a whole-time job. It demands both energy and leisure. Now energy and leisure are precisely the things which a hard worker lacks. Reduce his working hours and he will have both.

If, to-morrow or a couple of generations hence, it were made possible for all human beings to lead the life of leisure which is now led only by a few, the results, so far as I can see, would be as follows: There would be an enormous increase in the demand for such time-killers and substitutes for thought as newspapers, films, fiction, cheap means of communication and wireless telephones; to put it in more general terms, there would be an increase in the demand for sport and art. The interest in the fine art of love-making would be widely extended. And enormous numbers of people, hitherto immune from these mental and moral diseases, would be afflicted by ennui, depression and universal dissatisfaction.

The fact is that, brought up as they are at present, the majority of human beings can hardly fail to devote their leisure to occupations which, if not positively vicious, are at least stupid, futile and, what is worse, secretly realized to be futile.

To Tolstoy the whole idea of universal leisure seemed absurd and even wicked. The social reformers who held up the attainment of universal leisure as an ideal he regarded as madmen. They aspired to make all men like those rich, idle, urban people among whom he had passed his youth and whom he so profoundly despised. He regarded them as conspirators against the welfare of the race.

What seemed to Tolstoy important was not that the workers should get more leisure but that the leisured should work. For him the social ideal was labour for all in natural surroundings. He wanted to see all men and women living on the land and subsisting on the produce of the fields that they themselves had tilled. The makers of Utopias are fond of prophesying that a time will come when men will altogether abandon agriculture and live on synthetic foods; to Tolstoy the idea was utterly revolting. But though he was doubtless right to be revolted, the prophets of synthetic foods are probably better seers then he. Mankind is more likely to become urbanized than completely ruralized. But these probabilities do not concern us here. What concerns us is Tolstoy's opinion of leisure.

Tolstoy's dislike of leisure was due to his own experience as an idle youth and his observation of other rich and leisured men and women. He concluded that, as things are, leisure is generally more of a curse than a blessing. It is difficult, when one visits Monte Carlo or the other earthly paradises of the leisured, not to agree with him. Most minds will only do work under compulsion. Leisure is only profitable to those who desire, even without compulsion, to do mental work. In a society entirely composed of such active minds leisure would be an unmixed blessing. Such a society has never existed and does not at the present exist. Can it ever be called into being?

Those who believe that all the defects of nature may be remedied by suitable nurture will reply in the affirmative. And indeed it is sufficiently obvious that the science of education is still in a very rudimentary condition. We possess a sufficient knowledge of physiology to be able to devise gymnastic exercises that shall develop the body to its highest attainable efficiency. But our knowledge of the mind, and particularly of the growing mind, is far less complete; and even such knowledge as we possess is not systematically or universally applied to the problems of education. Our minds are like the flabby bodies of sedentary city dwellers—inefficient and imperfectly developed. With a vast number of people intellectual development ceases almost in childhood; they go through life with the intellectual capacities of boys or girls of fifteen. A proper course of mental gymnastics, based on real psychological knowledge, would at least permit all minds to reach their maximum development. Splendid prospect! But our enthusiasm for education is a little cooled when we consider what *is* the maximum development attainable by the greatest number of human beings. Men born with talents are to men born without them as human beings to dogs in respect to these particular faculties. Mathematically, I am a dog compared with Newton; a dog, musically, compared with Beethoven, and a dog, artistically, compared with Giotto. Not to mention the fact that I am a dog compared to Blondin, as a tight-rope walker; a billiard-playing dog compared with Newman; a boxing dog compared with Dempsey; a wine-tasting dog compared with Ruskin's father. And so on. Even if I were perfectly educated in mathematics, music, painting, tight-rope walking, billiard playing, boxing and wine-tasting, I should only become a trained dog instead of a dog in the state of nature. The prospect fills me with only moderate satisfaction.

Education can assure to every man the maximum of mental development. But is that maximum high enough in the majority of cases to allow a whole society to live in leisure without developing those deplorable qualities which have always characterized the leisured classes? I know plenty of people who have received the best education available in the present age and employ their leisure as though they had never been educated at all. But then our best education is admittedly bad (though good enough for all the men of talent and genius whom we possess); perhaps when it has been made really efficient, these people will spend their leisure contemplating the laws of nature. Perhaps. I venture to doubt it.

Mr Wells, who is a believer in nurture, puts his Utopia three thousand years into the future; Mr Shaw, less optimistically trusting to nature and a process of conscious evolution, removes his to the year 30,000 A.D. Geologically speaking, those times are to all intent equal in their brevity. Unfortunately, however, we are not fossils, but men. Even three thousand years seem, in our eyes, an uncommonly long time. The thought that, three thousand or thirty thousand years hence, human beings may, conceivably, be leading a lovely and rational existence is only mildly comforting and feebly sustaining. Men have a habit of thinking only of themselves, their children and their children's children. And they are quite right. Thirty thousand years hence, all may be well. But meanwhile that bad geological quarter of an hour which separates the present from that rosy future has got to be lived through. And I foresee that one of the minor, or even the major problems of that quarter of an hour will be the problem of leisure. By the year two thousand the six-hour day will be everywhere the rule, and the next hundred years will probably see the maximum reduced to five or even less. Nature, by then, will have had no time to change the mental habits of the race; and nurture, though improved, will only turn dogs into trained dogs. How will men and women fill their ever-expanding leisure? By contemplating the laws of nature, like Henri Poincaré? Or by reading the *News of the World*? I wonder.

BOOKS FOR THE JOURNEY

From *Along the Road* (1925)

ALL tourists cherish an illusion, of which no amount of experience can ever completely cure them; they imagine that they will find time, in the course of their travels, to do a lot of reading. They see themselves, at the end of a day's sight-seeing or motoring, or while they are sitting in the train, studiously turning over the pages of all the vast and serious works which, at ordinary seasons, they never find time to read. They start for a fortnight's tour in France, taking with them *The Critique of Pure Reason, Appearance and Reality*, the complete works of Dante and the *Golden Bough*. They come home to make the discovery that they have read something less than half a chapter of the *Golden Bough* and the first fifty-two lines of the *Inferno*. But that does not prevent them from taking just as many books the next time they set out on their travels.

Long experience has taught me to reduce in some slight measure the dimensions of my travelling library. But even now I am far too optimistic about my powers of reading while on a journey. Along with the books which I know it is possible to read, I still continue to put in a few impossible volumes in the pious hope that some day, somehow, they will get read. Thick tomes have travelled with me for thousands of kilometres across the face of Europe and have returned with their secrets unviolated. But whereas in the past I took nothing but thick tomes, and a great quantity of them at that, I now take only one or two and for the rest pack only the sort of books which I know by experience can be read in a hotel bedroom after a day's sight-seeing.

The qualities essential in a good travelling-book are these. It should be a work of such a kind that one can open it anywhere and be sure of finding something interesting, complete in itself and susceptible of being read in a short time. A book requiring continuous attention and prolonged mental effort is useless on a voyage; for leisure, when one travels, is brief and tinged with physical fatigue, the mind distracted and unapt to make protracted exertions.

Few travelling books are better than a good anthology of poetry in which every page contains something complete and perfect in itself. The brief respites from labour which the self-immolated tourist allows himself cannot be more delightfully filled than with the reading of poetry, which may even be got by heart; for the mind, though reluctant to follow an argument, takes pleasure in the slight labour of committing melodious words to memory.

In the choice of anthologies every traveller must please himself. My own favourite is Edward Thomas's *Pocket Book of Poems and Songs for the Open Air*. Thomas was a man of wide reading and of exquisite taste, and peculiarly gifted, moreover, to be an anthologist of the Open Air. For out of the huge tribe of modern versifiers who have babbled of green fields, Thomas is almost the only one whom one feels to be a 'nature poet' (the expression is somehow rather horrible, but there is no other) by right of birth and the conquest of real sympathy and understanding. It is not every one who says Lord, Lord, that shall enter into the kingdom of heaven; and few, very few of those who cry Cuckoo, Cuckoo, shall be admitted into the company of nature poets. For proof of this I refer my readers to the various volumes of Georgian Poetry.

Equally well adapted, with poetry, to the traveller's need, are collections of aphorisms or maxims. If they are good—and they must be very good indeed; for there is nothing more dismal than a 'Great Thought' enunciated by an author who has not himself the elements of greatness—maxims make the best of all reading. They take a minute to read and provide matter upon which thought can ruminate for hours. None are to be preferred to La Rochefoucauld's. Myself, I always reserve my upper left-hand waistcoat pocket for a small sexto-decimo reprint of the *Maximes*. It is a book to which there is no bottom or end. For with every month that one lives, with every accession to one's knowledge, both of oneself and of others, it means something more. For La Rochefoucauld knew almost everything about the human soul, so that practically every discovery one can make oneself, as one advances through life, has been anticipated by him and formulated in the briefest and most elegant phrases. I say advisedly that La Rochefoucauld knew 'almost' everything about the human soul; for it is obvious that he did not know all. He knew everything about the souls of human beings in so far as they are social animals. Of the soul of man in solitude—of man when he is no more interested in the social pleasures and successes which were, to La Rochefoucauld, so all-important—he knows little or nothing. If we desire to know something about the human soul in solitude—in its relations, not to man, but to God—we must go elsewhere: to the Gospels, to the novels of Dostoievsky, for example. But man in his social relationships has never been more accurately described, and his motives never more delicately analysed than by La Rochefoucauld. The aphorisms vary considerably in value; but the best of them—and their number is surprisingly large—are astonishingly profound and pregnant. They resume a vast experience. In a sentence La Rochefoucauld compresses as much material as would serve a novelist for a long story. Conversely, it would not surprise me to learn that many novelists turn to the *Maximes* for suggestions for plots and characters. It is impossible, for example, to read Proust without being reminded of the *Maximes*, or the *Maximes* without being reminded of Proust. 'Le plaisir de l'amour est d'aimer, et l'on est plus heureux par la passion que l'on a que par celle que l'on donne.' 'Il y a des gens si remplis d'eux-mêmes, que, lorsqu'ils sont amoureux, ils trouvent moyen d'être occupés de leur passion sans l'être de la personne qu'ils aiment.' What are all the love stories in *A la Recherche du Temps Perdu* but enormous amplifications of these aphorisms? Proust is La Rochefoucauld magnified ten thousand times.

Hardly less satisfactory as travel books are the aphoristic works of Nietzsche. Nietzsche's sayings have this in common with La

Rochefoucauld's, that they are pregnant and expansive. His best aphorisms are long trains of thought, compressed. The mind can dwell on them at length because so much is implicit on them. It is in this way that good aphorisms differ from mere epigrams, in which the whole point consists in the felicity of expression. An epigram pleases by surprising; after the first moment the effect wears off and we are no further interested in it. One is not taken in twice by the same practical joke. But an aphorism does not depend on verbal wit. Its effect is not momentary, and the more we think of it, the more substance we find in it.

Another excellent book for a journey—for it combines expansive aphorisms with anecdotes—is Boswell's *Life of Johnson*, which the Oxford Press now issues, on India paper, in a single small octavo volume. (All travellers, by the way, owe much to the exertions of Henry Frowde, of the Oxford Press, the inventor, or at least the European reinventor, of that fine rag paper, impregnated with mineral matter to give it opacity, which we call India paper.) What the aphorism is to the philosophical treatise, the India paper volume is to the ponderous editions of the past. All Shakespeare, perfectly legible, gets into a volume no bigger than a single novel by the late Charles Garvice. All Pepys, or as much of him as the British public is allowed to read, can now be fitted into three pockets. And the Bible, reduced to an inch in thickness, must surely be in danger of losing those bullet-stopping qualities which it used, at any rate in romantic novels, to possess. Thanks to Henry Frowde one can get a million words of reading matter into a rucksack and hardly feel the difference in its weight.

India paper and photography have rendered possible the inclusion in a portable library of what in my opinion is the best traveller's book of all—a volume (any one of the thirty-two will do) of the twelfth, half-size edition of the *Encyclopaedia Britannica*. It takes up very little room (eight and a half inches by six and a half by one is not excessive), it contains about a thousand pages and an almost countless number of curious and improbable facts. It can be dipped into anywhere, its component chapters are complete in themselves and not too long. For the traveller, disposing as he does only of brief half-hours, it is the perfect book, the more so, since I take it that, being a born traveller, he is likely also to be one of those desultory and self-indulgent readers to whom the *Encyclopaedia*, when not used for some practical purpose, must specially appeal. I never pass a day away from home without taking a volume with me. It is the book of books. Turning over its pages, rummaging among the stores of fantastically varied facts which the hazards of alphabetical arrangement bring together, I wallow in my mental vice. A stray volume of the *Encyclopaedia* is like the mind of a learned madman —stored with correct ideas, between which, however, there is no other connection than the fact that there is a B in both; from orach, or mountain spinach, one passes directly to oracles. That one does not oneself go mad, or become, in the process of reading the *Encyclopaedia*, a mine of useless and unrelated knowledge is due to the fact that one forgets. The mind has a vast capacity for oblivion. Providentially; otherwise, in the chaos of futile memories, it would be impossible to remember anything useful or coherent. In practice, we work with generalizations, abstracted out of the turmoil of realities. If we remembered everything perfectly, we should never be able to generalize at all; for there would appear before our minds nothing but individual images, precise and different. Without ignorance we could not generalize. Let us thank Heaven for our powers of forgetting. With regard to the *Encyclopaedia*, they are enormous. The mind only remembers that of which it has some need. Five minutes after reading about mountain spinach, the ordinary man, who is neither a botanist nor a cook, has forgotten all about it. Read for amusement, the *Encyclopaedia* serves only to distract for the moment; it does not instruct, it deposits nothing on the surface of the mind that will remain. It is a mere time-killer and momentary tickler of the mind. I use it only for amusement on my travels; I should be ashamed to indulge so wantonly in mere curiosity at home, during seasons of serious business.

CAWNPORE

From *Jesting Pilate* (1926)

EDWARD LEAR has a rhyme about

> an old man of Thermopylae,
> Who never did anything properly.

To the Westerner all Indians seem old men of Thermopylae. In the ordinary affairs of life I am a bit of a Thermopylean myself. But even I am puzzled, disquieted, and rather exasperated by the Indians. To a thoroughly neat-minded and efficient man, with a taste for tidiness and strong views about respectability and the keeping up of appearances, Indians must be literally maddening.

It would be possible to compile a long and varied list of what I may call Indian Thermopylisms. But I prefer to confine my attention to the Thermopylean behaviour of Indians in a single sphere of activity—that of ceremonial. For it is, I think, in matters of ceremonial and the keeping up of appearances that Indians most conspicuously fail, in our Western opinion, 'to do anything properly.' Nobody who has looked into a temple or witnessed the ceremonies of an Indian marriage can fail to have been struck by the extraordinary 'sloppiness' and inefficiency of the symbolical performances. The sublime is constantly alternated with the ridiculous and trivial, and the most monstrous incongruities are freely mingled. The old man of Thermopylae is as busy in the palace as in the temple; and the abodes of Indian potentates are an incredible mixture of the magnificent and the cheap, the grandiose and the ludicrously homely. Cows bask on the front steps; the anteroom is filthy with the droppings of pigeons; beggars doze under the gates, or search one another's heads for lice; in one of the inner courts fifty courtesans from the city are singing interminable songs in honour of the birth of the Maharaja's eleventh grandchild; in the throne room, nobody

41

quite knows why, there stands a brass bedstead with a sham mahogany wardrobe from the Tottenham Court Road beside it; framed colour prints from the Christmas number of the *Graphic* of 1907 alternate along the walls with the most exquisite Rajput and Persian miniatures; in the unswept jewel room, five million pounds' worth of precious stones lies indiscriminately heaped; the paintings are peeling off the walls of the private apartments, a leprosy has attacked the stucco, there is a hole in the carpet; the marble hall of audience is furnished with bamboo chairs, and the Rolls Royces are driven by ragged chauffeurs who blow their noses on the long and wind-blown end of their turbans. As an Englishman belonging to that impecunious but dignified section of the upper middle-class which is in the habit of putting on dress-clothes to eat—with the most studied decorum and out of porcelain and burnished silver—a dinner of dishwater and codfish, mock duck and cabbage, I was always amazed, I was pained and shocked by this failure on the part of Eastern monarchs to keep up appearances, and do what is owing to their position.

I was even more helplessly bewildered by the Thermopylean behaviour of the delegates at the Cawnpore Congress during Mr Gandhi's speech on the position of Indians in South Africa. The applause when he ascended the rostrum was loud—though rather less loud than a Western observer might have expected. Indian audiences are not much given to yelling or hand-clapping, and it is not possible, when one is sitting on the floor, to stamp one's feet. But though the noise was small, the enthusiasm was evidently very great. And yet, when the Mahatma began to speak, there was more talking and fidgeting, more general in-attention than during any other speech of the day. True, it was late in the afternoon when Mr Gandhi made his speech. The delegates had spent a long and hungry day sitting on a floor that certainly grew no softer with the passage of the hours. There was every reason for their feeling the need to relax their minds and stretch their cramped legs. But however acute its weariness had become, a Western audience would surely have postponed the moment of relaxation until the great man had finished speaking. Even if it had found the speech boring, it would have felt itself bound to listen silently and with attention to a great and admired national hero. It would have considered that chattering and fidgeting were signs of disrespect. Not so, evidently, the Indian audience. To show disrespect for the Mahatma was probably the last thing in the world that the Cawnpore delegates desired. Nevertheless they talked all through the speech, they stretched their stiff legs, they called for water, they went out for little strolls in the Congress grounds and came back, noisily. Knowing how Englishmen could comport themselves during a speech by a national hero, combining in his single person the sanctity of the Archbishop of Canterbury with the popularity of the Prince of Wales, I was astonished, I was profoundly puzzled.

In an earlier entry in this diary I attributed the Thermopylism of the Indians to a certain emotional agility (shared, to some extent, by the natives of Southern Europe), to a capacity for feeling two things at once or, at least, in very rapid succession. Indians and Neapolitans, I pointed out, can reverence their gods even while spitting, jesting, and picking their noses. But this explanation does not go far enough; it requires itself to be explained. How is it that, while we are brought up to practise consistency of behaviour, the children of other races are educated so as to be emotionally agile? Why are we so carefully taught to keep up the appearances which to others seem so negligible?

Reflecting on my observations in Italy and in India, I am led to believe that these questions must be answered in one way for the Southern Europeans, in another for the Indians. The emotional agility of the Italians is due to the profound 'realism' of their outlook, coupled with their ingrained habit of judging things in terms of aesthetics. Thus, the Southern European may admire a religious service or a royal procession as works of art, while holding strong atheistical and anti-monarchial opinions; he will be able to mock and to admire simultaneously. And perhaps he is not an atheist or a republican at all. But however ardently a Christian or a monarchist, he will always find himself able to reflect—while he kneels before the elevated Host or cheers the royal barouche—that the priest and the king make a very good thing out of their business and that they are, after all, only human, like himself—probably all too human. As for the shabbinesses and absurdities of the performance, he will ignore them in his appreciation of the grandiose intention, the artistic general effect. And he will regard the Northerner who wants the performance to be perfect in every detail as a laborious and unimaginative fool. Nor will he understand the Northerner's passion for keeping up appearances in ordinary daily life. The Southerner has a liking for display; but his display is different from ours. When we go in for keeping up appearances, we do the job, not showily, but thoroughly, and at every point. We want all the rooms in our house to look 'nice', we want everything in it to be 'good'; we train our servants to behave as nearly as possible like automatons, and we put on special clothes to eat even the worst of dinners. The Southerner, on the other hand concentrates his display into a single splendid flourish. He likes to get something spectacular for his money, and his aim is to achieve, not respectability, but a work of art. He gives his house a splendid façade, trusting that every lover of the grandiose will be content to contemplate the marble front, without peering too closely at the brick and rubble behind. He will furnish one drawing-room in style, for state occasions. To keep up appearances at every point—for oneself and one's servants, as well as for the outside world—seems to him a folly and a waste of spirit. Life is meant to be enjoyed, and occasional grandiosities are part of the fun. But on ordinary days of the week it is best enjoyed in shirt sleeves.

The Indian's Thermopylisms are due, it seems to me, to entirely different causes. He is careless about keeping up appearances, because appearances seem to him as nothing in comparison with 'spiritual reality'. He is slack in the performance of anything in the nature of symbolic ceremonial, because the invisible thing symbolized seems to him so much more important than the symbol. He is a Thermopylean, not through excess of 'realism' and the aesthetic sense, but through excess of 'spirituality'. Thus the Maharaja does not trouble to make his surroundings look princely, because he feels that princeliness lies within him, not without. Marriages are made in heaven; therefore it is unnecessary to take trouble about mere marriage ceremonies on earth. And if the soul of every Indian is overflowing with love and respect for Mahatma Gandhi, why should Congress delegates trouble to give that respect the merely physical form of silence and motionlessness?

Such arguments, of course, are never consciously put. But the training of Indians is such that they act as though in obedience to them. They have been taught that this present world is more or less illusory, that the aim of every man should be to break out of the cycle of recurrent birth, that the 'soul' is everything and that the highest values are purely 'spiritual'. Owing to their early inculcation, such beliefs have tended to become almost instinctive, even in the minds of those whose consciously formulated philosophy of life is of an entirely different character. It is obvious that people holding such beliefs will attach the smallest importance to the keeping up of appearances.

In these matters we Northerners behave like Behaviourists—as though the visible or audible expression of an idea were the idea itself, as though the symbol in some sort created the notion symbolized. Our religious rites, our acts of 'natural piety', are solemnly performed, and with an almost military precision. The impressive service, we have found, actually manufactures God; the memorial ceremony creates and conserves our interest in the dead. Our royal pageantry is no less rich, no less consistently effective; for the pageant *is* the king. Our judges are wigged and magnificently robed. Absurd survival! But no; the majesty of the law consists in the wigs and the ermine. The gentry keeps up appearances to the limit of its financial means and beyond. It is a folly, protests the believer in 'spiritual' realities. On the contrary, it is profound wisdom, based on the instinctive recognition of a great historical truth. History shows us that there were rites before there were dogmas, that there were conventions of behaviour before there was morality. Dogmas, indeed, have often been the children of rites—systems of thought called into existence to explain gestures. Morality is the theory of pre-existing social habits. (In the same way some of the greatest advances in mathematics have been due to the invention of symbols, which it afterwards became necessary to explain; from the minus sign proceeded the whole theory of negative quantities.) To sceptics desirous of believing, catholic directors of conscience prescribe the outward and visible practice of religion; practice, they know, brings forth faith; the formal appearance of religion creates its 'spiritual' essence. It is the same with civilization; men who practise the conventional ritual of civilization become civilized. Appearing to be civilized, they really are so. For civilization is nothing but a series of conventions; being civilized is obeying those conventions, is keeping up the appearances of culture, prosperity, and good manners. The more widely and the more efficiently such appearances are kept up, the better the civilisation. There can never be a civilization that ignores appearances and is wholly 'spiritual'. A civilization based on Quaker principles could not come into existence; Quakerism in all its forms is the product, by reaction, of a civilization already highly developed. Before one can ignore appearances and conventions, there must be, it is obvious, conventions and appearances to ignore. The Simple Life is simple only in comparison with some existing life of complicated convention. If Quaker principles ceased to be the luxury of a refined few, and were accepted by the world at large, civilization would soon cease to exist: freed from the necessity of keeping up the appearance of being civilized, the majority of human beings would rapidly become barbarous.

Admirers of India are unanimous in praising Hindu 'spirituality'. I cannot agree with them. To my mind 'spirituality' (ultimately, I suppose, the product of the climate) is the primal curse of India and the cause of all her misfortunes. It is this preoccupation with 'spiritual' realities, different from the actual historical realities of common life, that has kept millions upon millions of men and women content, through centuries, with a lot unworthy of human beings. A little less spirituality, and the Indians would now be free—free from foreign dominion and from the tyranny of their own prejudices and traditions. There would be less dirt and more food. There would be fewer Maharajas with Rolls Royces and more schools. The women would be out of their prisons, and there would be some kind of polite and conventional social life—one of those despised appearances of civilization which are yet the very stuff and essence of civilized existence. At a safe distance and from the midst of a network of sanitary plumbing, Western observers, disgusted, not unjustifiably, with their own civilization, express their admiration for the 'spirituality' of the Indians, and for the immemorial contentment which is the fruit of it. Sometimes, such is their enthusiasm, this admiration actually survives a visit to India.

It is for its 'materialism' that our Western civilization is generally blamed. Wrongly, I think. For materialism—if materialism means a preoccupation with the actual world in which we live—is something wholly admirable. If Western civilization is unsatisfactory, that is not because we are interested in the actual world; it is because the majority of us are interested in such an absurdly small part of it. Our world is wide, incredibly varied and more fantastic than any product of the imagination. And yet the lives of the vast majority of men and women among the Western peoples are narrow, monotonous, and dull. We are not materialistic enough; that is the trouble. We do not interest ourselves in a sufficiency of this marvellous world of ours. Travel is cheap and rapid; the immense accumulations of modern knowledge lie heaped up on every side. Every man with a little leisure and enough money for railway tickets, every man, indeed, who knows how to read, has it in his power to magnify himself, to multiply the ways in which he exists, to make his life full, significant, and interesting. And yet, for some inexplicable reason, most of us prefer to spend our leisure and our surplus energies in elaborately, brainlessly, and expensively murdering time. Our lives are consequently barren and uninteresting, and we are, in general, only too acutely conscious of the fact. The remedy is more materialism and not, as false prophets from the East assert, more 'spirituality'—more interest in this world, not in the other. The Other World—the world of metaphysics and religion—can never possibly be as interesting as this world, and for an obvious reason. The Other World is an invention of the human fancy and shares the limitations of its creator. This world, on the other hand, the world of the materialists, is the fantastic and incredible invention of—well, not in any case of Mrs Annie Besant.

EDUCATION

From *Proper Studies* (1927)

OUR educational policy is based on two enormous fallacies. The first is that which regards the intellect as a box inhabited by autonomous ideas, whose numbers can be increased by the simple process of opening the lid of the box and introducing new ideas. The second fallacy is, that all minds are alike and can profit by the same system of training. All official systems of education are systems for pumping the same knowledge by the same methods into radically different minds. Minds being living organisms, not dustbins, irreducibly dissimilar and not uniform, the official systems of education are not, as might be expected, particularly successful. That the hopes of the ardent educationists of the democratic epoch will ever be fulfilled seems extremely doubtful. Great men cannot be made to order by any system of training, however perfect. The most that we can hope to do is to train every individual to realize all his potentialities and become completely himself. But the self of one individual will be Shakespeare's self, the self of another Flecknoe's. The prevailing systems of education not only fail to turn Flecknoes into Shakespeares (no system of education will ever do that); they fail to make the best of the Flecknoes. Flecknoe is not given a chance to become even himself. Congenitally a sub-man, he is condemned by education to spend his life as a sub-sub-man.

OUR DEBT TO THE IMBECILES

Before embarking on any speculations about the ideal and possible future systems of education, it is necessary to give some account of the existing system and of the reforms in it which have already been made.

It is to the imbeciles and the mentally deficient that we owe such reforms as have been made in the old systems of education. If the mind is a mere receptacle which can be filled mechanically, as one fills a jug with water, it follows that a child who does not learn remains ignorant only through lack of good will; he deliberately closes his mental box, he refuses, malignantly, to admit the knowledge which his teachers are trying to pump into it. There is only one remedy: he must be compelled to open his mind; the opposing will must be broken—by moral persuasion, by threats, by physical torture. The fine old system of mechanical repetitive teaching, tempered by flagellation, was developed and perfected through the centuries.

No systematic effort was made in the past to teach the mentally deficient. They were left in the full enjoyment of their imbecility. The more eccentric lunacies received medical treatment, which consisted of a combination of imprisonment, starving, and beating. This system was designed to drive out the devils, by whom our Bible-reading ancestors imagined all madmen to be possessed. With the growth of that strange new spirit which we call humanitarianism there arose a new sense of responsibility towards these unfortunate beings. Efforts were made to lift them out of their imbecility, to educate them up towards normality. As soon as this effort was seriously made, it became manifest that the current methods of educating normal children were entirely inadequate and unsuitable when applied to deficients. It was obvious that, if imbeciles could not learn, it was not through any malignant refusal to admit knowledge; it was through inability. They could not be flogged into opening the doors of their mental boxes, they could not be bullied into learning uninteresting things by rote; but they could, it was gradually found, be persuaded, be stimulated and amused into acquiring some kinds of knowledge. They remained deficients; but at least they were now deficients who had been educated up to the limits of their native capacity.

Imbeciles are not different in kind from normal folk only in degree. Between the idiot and the man of exceptional ability stretches an unbroken series of graded types. The method of teaching which is found suitable for the lowest type will be suitable—with proper modifications—for the highest. If the best

way of teaching deficients is to interest them in what they have
to learn, then that is also the best way of teaching the normally
and abnormally intelligent. It pays to treat the minds of idiots
as though they were delicate living organisms requiring careful
nurture; it does not pay to teach mechanically, even when such
teaching is backed by threats and flagellation. Imbeciles cannot
learn, even after countless repetitions, the things which do not
interest them. The same applies to more intelligent children.
True, they are intelligent enough to learn something, even when
the teaching is dull, mechanically repetitive, and brutal. But they
would learn more if they were taught by the same methods
(*mutatis mutandis*) as have proved successful in the training of
imbeciles.

The helplessness of very small children, their incapacity to
think and will as adults do, are almost as manifest as the helplessness and incapacity of deficients. Indeed, a deficient may be
regarded as one whose mind has never grown up, so that when
his chronological and corporeal age is, shall we say, ten years, his
mental age is only two. The methods of teaching this abnormal
child of ten will therefore be entirely suitable when applied to the
normal child of two. The obvious resemblance of the deficient to
the infantile mind has led to great reforms in the organized
teaching of small children. The education of infants in Kinder-
gartens, Montessori Schools, or Macmillan Nursery Schools com-
pares favourably with even the best systems of training devised
for larger children. To the systems of mechanical education
current in our ordinary schools it is incomparably superior.
Where the official systems ignore psychological facts, infant education, as developed in the best modern schools, is realistically
scientific. Where they create misery, boredom, an insubordina-
tion requiring rigorous repression, and a hatred of learning, it
spreads joy, self-discipline, and the eager desire for knowledge.

TRAINING OF INFANTS

There are many kinds of infant schools; but all are conducted
on fundamentally the same principles. The aim of all of them is

to teach the child to teach himself. First of all, the senses are trained. Playing, the child is given practice in seeing, hearing, touching, smelling. This training of the senses is of the highest importance. Sensuous impressions are the basis of all mental processes; the more things we have touched, seen, heard, the richer will be our imagination, the more we shall have to think about, and the greater the number of ways in which we shall be able to think. Further, the process of exercising the sense stimulates the whole infantile mind, strengthens it and quickens its growth. Imbecile children given exercise in the handling of objects have developed and improved. Left to themselves or to the mercy of untrained parents—whose love is only equalled by their total ignorance and ineptitude in the matter of education—children receive a most inadequate sensuous training, especially if brought up in the drab and sordid environment of a city. The systematic training of the senses is of vital importance to every town-bred child.

Sensuous training is combined with handwork, which at this early age is necessarily of the simplest and most rudimentary kind. Much ingenious apparatus has been devised for the child to train his fingers on. But learning to dress is in itself an education—a better one, perhaps, than learning to do things with much more elaborate and far-fetched apparatus than laces and buttons. For clothes are near and important to the child, and it is through that which is immediately significant to the learner that all education should begin. Few adults and practically no children are interested in abstract things, or, for that matter, in anything outside the circle of their immediate experience. To teach a number of 'subjects', entirely unrelated to their daily lives, is to guarantee for your pupils inevitable boredom, a difficult learning, and an all too easy forgetting. Children should learn as the human race learned; they should set out from the immediate and the concrete to discover the abstract, the general and the remote. History and geography should begin with the family and the native place. The sciences must blossom out of the local flowers, must be born with the familiar animals, spring from the neighbouring rocks and waters, be deduced from the practice of the local crafts and industries. Geometry must arise as it arose among the Egyptians—from the measurement for practical purposes of definite individual spaces. Arithmetic must solve the actual problems of daily life. And so on. Higher education is so remote from ordinary life that it hardly affects the majority of learners. Most of our contemporary Babbitts have been to the university. A higher education that turns out such products must indeed be in need of reform. The interests, the intellectual outlook, of the educated Babbitt are exactly the same as those of the uneducated. This means only one thing: the various 'subjects' taught at our educational establishments are so completely disconnected with life that it never even occurs to the learners to absorb them into the practical workaday part of their minds; it never even strikes them that knowledge may be used to enrich ordinary experience, to test prejudices and conventions of conduct. Philosophy, science, literature are so many 'subjects', learned and forgotten. The essential Babbitt remains unmodified by them. He emerges from the university the unregenerate Philistine he was before he entered. If knowledge is to be loved for its own sake, if it is to affect the conduct of the generality of mankind (as it is essential in this rapidly changing modern world that it should), it is necessary—for most adults and adolescents as well as for all children—that what is now abstract and remote should be wedded in some way to practical life, that it should be made to spring from the ordinary experiences of modern man, and so be enabled to modify his conduct.

In the best infant schools this synthesis of knowledge and practical life is an accomplished fact. An analogous synthesis of the vastly more complicated knowledge imparted in the course of higher education and the practical interests of adolescents and adults must be made. The need is urgent. If we go on as we are doing now, we shall not merely fail to profit by the immense accumulations of knowledge which a few eccentric historical researchers and men of science have piled up; we shall carry our civilization headlong to disaster. A twentieth-century material civilization cannot be worked by people whose minds are predominantly mediaeval or even prehistoric.

The training of the imagination follows and accompanies the later stages of the sensuous training of small children. Children are encouraged to make things for themselves, to act, to make believe, to tell stories. The powers of self-expression are strengthened by this practice; the child learns confidence in himself. Moreover, the teacher takes care to direct the children's play into educational channels. She sees to it that the children's games of make-believe take the form of pretending to be prehistoric men, Romans, ancient Britons—it is a history lesson. Playing with mud and sticks and water, they make islands, lakes, mountains, rivers; they are learning geography. They are told and then re-tell, act over, stories from fable and history. Speaking and acting dissipate shyness, give control of the voice and gestures, and enable the children, by actually living their literature, to understand it to the full. The reading of Shakespeare forms a part of the ordinary curriculum of English-speaking school children. Read in the ordinary way by a class of children sitting at desks, out of a horrid little school edition provided with the sort of notes that one can be examined on, a play by Shakespeare seems meaningless and dull. Naturally; Shakespeare did not write his plays to be read, with notes, by children sitting at desks; he wrote them to be acted. Children who have read the plays dramatically, who have lived through them with their whole imaginative being, acquire an understanding of Shakespeare, a feeling for the poetry, denied to those who have ploughed through them in class and passed, even with honours, an examination in the notes.

No teacher of small children should attempt too early to teach anything requiring sustained flights of abstract logical reasoning. In the vast majority of children the logical faculty develops late; small children, like savages, do not admit the cogency of logic. The powers of ratiocination should be exercised in following trains of argument, which must be progressively lengthened, as the feeling for logic grows, from the shortest possible piece of pure reasoning to the longest each pupil is able to follow. And in all cases, as we have seen, these exercises in pure ratiocination should start from the near, concrete, and therefore interesting fact.

THE OFFICIAL SYSTEM COMES INTO ACTION

From the infant school (if he has had the luck to be sent to one instead of being brought up by incompetent parents or nurses) the child must pass to an elementary or preparatory school. The change is, in almost every case, profoundly for the worse. The methods of instruction current at a good infant school are psychologically sound. At the ordinary boys' or girls' school the education is founded on a psychological fallacy, and the child is too often regarded as existing for the System, not the System for the child. At this school and at others exactly resembling it in spirit and in educational methods the child must remain until the times comes for him—if it ever does come—to go to the university. There, if he has the luck to go to the right kind of university, he will once more be receiving education of a reasonable and decent sort. He may, on the contrary, go to a bad university, in which most of the vices of the unreformed schools are stupidly perpetuated. In that case, he will go out into the world without ever having known, except during a few years of early childhood, what a proper education is. The astonishing thing is that he contrives to learn as much as he does. That he could, if taught in the right way, be made into a much better and more intelligent citizen than he becomes under the present system, one cannot doubt. But it may be remarked parenthetically that the absurd and irrational systems of education under which they were brought up have not in the past prevented men and women of outstanding talent from fully developing their powers. In spite of no education, in spite of what is worse, mechanical and brutal education, they have been themselves, they have done their work. They were too strong for their environment: they educated themselves. Ordinary folk succumb to their environment. They suffer themselves to be taught (which is all that most educationists want them to do), and so become what the system makes them, dim, incurious people, not desiring knowledge, and quite ignorant of the way in which knowledge may be obtained if it should ever be needed. What is required is a system of education which shall encourage boys and girls (not merely infants, as is at present the case) to teach themselves; a system calculated to foster the child's curiosity through all the years of growth, to make the desire for knowledge a chronic and habitual desire, and to familiarize each child with the best methods of acquiring it by his own efforts. What is needed, in a word, is a system of individual education.

Let us briefly trace the career of the growing school child. In the infant school, if he was lucky enough to attend one, he was taught to teach himself, to develop his own faculties, to use his senses and his imagination—the herald, as Goethe called it, and indeed the parent of his reason. His education was an active one. In the higher schools, to which he is now promoted, the education is mainly passive. No longer is he expected to use initiative, to discover things for himself. His first duty is now to sit still and let the school master or mistress teach him. He is regarded as an empty vessel. The function of the teacher is to fill him. In the infant school, on the contrary, he was regarded as a living, developing organism, and the teacher was there to create an appetite in him for knowledge and virtue, to make truth, beauty, and goodness tempting, and to show him the best way of acquiring these things by his own efforts. A great gulf separates the two schools.

In the higher schools the child finds himself a member of a class—of a very large class in most schools, except those of the rich. (And even in these—I am thinking in particular of the English Public Schools—the classes are sometimes fantastically large.) There may be forty, fifty, even sixty children with him in the same room. His talents are expected to conform to the average standard of this assemblage. He may be exceptionally clever and quick, or exceptionally slow and dull. In either case he is a nuisance to his teacher and to his fellow pupils, and in either case his own education suffers. If he is clever, he is held back by the majority of ordinary boys. If he is stupid, he is dragged along so fast that it is impossible for him to learn anything completely and thoroughly. Passively, with his forty or fifty dissimilar and unique companions, he sits at his desk while the teacher pumps and mechanically re-pumps information into his mental receptacle.

> Ram it in, ram it in!
> Children's heads are hollow.
> Ram it in, ram it in!
> Still there's more to follow.

If the teacher is a severe disciplinarian, the child will sit still and at any rate appear to drink in his words. If the teacher is lax, he will more frankly day-dream, scribble, fidget, openly play the fool. Satan, we know on good authority, finds work for idle hands to do. While the teacher is discoursing, the child is necessarily idle, passive, unoccupied. Moreover, the lesson is generally dull and has to be constantly repeated, owing to the incapacity of a young mind to fix its attention on anything that does not interest it. Each repetition makes the lesson slightly duller. Even the work which the children have to do for themselves—sums, translations, answers to questions referring to the last history or geography lesson, and so on—cannot truly be called occupation. For such tasks are too often no more than meaningless exercises, unrelated to anything in the child's experience and performed for their own silly sake, because the teacher has said that they must be performed, without interest or desire. In how different a spirit will a child undertake a task, even the most arduous, which he feels to be significant and important! Plunged in such work—work he can really see the sense of—he will be really and truly occupied. Satan will find no extra work of mischief for him to do, and the question of discipline will simply not arise. But of this later.

THE DANGERS OF GOOD TEACHING

Hitherto we have been considering the uninspired teacher, who works his or her way dully and mechanically through the prescribed curriculum. But teachers may be, and frequently are, charming, intelligent, and persuasive. They may put things well; they may speak in a way that will command attention and awake emotion and enthusiasm; they may have a power of making difficulties seem easy. The child will listen to such teachers and will greatly appreciate them—particularly if he has an examination to pass in the near future. But the more accomplished a teacher is in the art of lecturing or coaching, the worse he is as an educator. Working on the old-fashioned system, the clever teacher (deplorable paradox!) does almost more harm than the stupid one. For the clever schoolmaster makes things too easy for his pupils; he relieves them of the necessity of finding out things for themselves. By dint of brilliant teaching he succeeds in almost eliminating the learning process. He knows how to fill his pupils with ready-made knowledge, which they inevitably forget (since it is not *their* knowledge and cost them nothing to acquire) as soon as the examination for which it was required is safely passed. The stupid teacher, on the other hand, may be so completely intolerable that the child will perhaps be driven, despairingly and in mere self-defence, to educate himself; in which case the incompetent shepherd will have done, all unwittingly, a great service to his charge, by forcing him into a rebellious intellectual independence.

MASS EDUCATION

The defects of the ordinary system of mass education are so enormous that it is hardly necessary to expatiate on them any further. They may be briefly summarized as follows. First, the system of teaching in large classes is intolerant and rigid. No allowance is made for the idiosyncrasies of the individual child, who is sacrificed to the average of the class. The class and the fixed curriculum are like the bed of Procrustes in the myth;

those who are too long for the bed are cut down until they fit; those who are too short are stretched. The child who is quick and talented in one subject but not in others (and every human being has his special gifts) is compelled under the current system of mass education to sacrifice his talents to his deficiencies. Thus a child may have a great talent for English and none for arithmetic. He may be endowed with a real feeling for literature, a gift of composition; but when you ask him what percentage of a floor 18.7 feet long by $5\frac{3}{16}$ metres wide remains uncovered when you have spent three pounds eleven shillings and sevenpence three farthings plus 26 rupees 12 annas on linoleum costing $179.06 per acre, he finds it difficult or impossible to reply. He must therefore remain in a low class, where they read nothing but baby books and concentrate on spelling and grammar until such time as he can solve this interesting and instructive problem.

Second, under the present system of mass education by classes too much stress is laid on teaching and too little on active learning. The child is not encouraged to discover things on his own account. He learns to rely on outside help, not on his own powers, thus losing intellectual independence and all capacity to judge for himself. The over-taught child is the father of the newspaper-reading, advertisement-believing, propaganda-swallowing, demagogue-led man—the man who makes modern democracy the farce it is. Moreover, lessons in class leave him mainly unoccupied, and therefore bored. He has to be coerced into learning what does not interest him, and the information acquired mechanically and reluctantly, by dint of brute repetition, is rapidly forgotten.

Third, the child, being bored and unoccupied, is also mischievous. A strict external discipline becomes necessary, unless there is to be chaos and pandemonium. The child learns to obey, not to control himself. He loses moral as well as intellectual independence.

Such are the main defects in the current system of mass education. Many others could be mentioned; but they are defects in detail and can be classified under one or other of the three main categories of defects—sacrifice of the individual to the system, psychologically unsound methods of teaching, and irrational methods of imposing discipline. We need a new system of universal education of the same kind as that which has proved itself so successful in the training of defectives and infants, but modified so as to be suitable for older boys and girls. We need, as I have said in an earlier paragraph, a system of individual education.

POLITICAL DEMOCRACY

From *Proper Studies* (1927)

THE DEMOCRATIC CREED

MR CHESTERTON has been eloquent, among so many other things, about democracy. And since his eloquence is also a lucid profession of the faith that is in political democrats, I shall brighten a page with a rather long quotation from his admirable *Orthodoxy*. 'This is the first principle of democracy,' writes Mr Chesterton: 'that the essential thing in men are the things they hold in common, not the things they hold separately. And the second principle is merely this: that the political instinct or desire is one of these things which they hold in common. Falling in love is more poetical than dropping into poetry. The democratic contention is that government (helping to rule the tribe) is a thing like falling in love, and not a thing like dropping into poetry. It is not something analogous to playing the church organ, painting on vellum, discovering the North Pole, looping the loop, being Astronomer Royal, and so on. For these things we do not wish a man to do at all, unless he does them well. It is, on the contrary, a thing analogous to writing one's own love letters or blowing one's own nose. These things we want a man to do for himself even if he does them badly. I am not here arguing the truth of any of these conceptions; I know that some moderns are asking to have their wives chosen by scientists, and they may soon be asking, for all I know, to have their noses blown by nurses. I merely say that mankind does recognize these universal human functions, and that democracy classes government among them. In short, the democratic faith is this, that the most terribly important things must be left to ordinary men themselves—the mating of the sexes, the rearing of the young, the laws of the state. This is democracy; and in this I have always believed.'

There is something very engaging about Mr Chesterton's mixture of frankness and sophistry. He professes a chronic and unshakable faith in conceptions which he admits are quite probably not true. 'I am not here arguing about the truth of any of these conceptions,' he says, with an honesty which does him enormous credit. But he then goes on to confuse the issue by talking about vicariously chosen wives and delegated nose-blowing. We are led by this rhetorical device to discount the previous admission. So few people want their wives chosen and their noses blown by some one else, that their existence may be ignored. The implication is that we may also safely ignore the existence of the equally small number of people who do not want to do their own governing. The truth is, of course, that the people who do not want to choose their own wives or blow their own noses are infinitely rarer than the people who do not want to take a share in 'ruling the tribe'. Mr Chesterton began admitting the fact, but changed his mind half-way and decided to mitigate the frankness of his confession. He had begun to say something like this: 'I think that all men *ought* to take an interest in government, and I think so passionately in spite of the fact that, in practice, most of them take no interest whatever in the matter.' But since a frank and full statement of the fact would have made nonsense of his political ideal—for a statesman's notion of what ought to be is merely silly and academic if it does not stand in some sort of living relationship with what is—he checked himself half-way, and having admitted that his ideal might not necessarily rhyme with the facts, proceeded to imply that, after all, it did rhyme more or less.

THE DEMOCRATIC FACTS

All observation, however, tends to show that this particular conception of what ought to be has very little connection with the things that are. Men ought, no doubt, to take an interest in law-making and the rule of the nation. (And here let me remark parenthetically that Mr Chesterton's use of the word 'tribe' instead of 'nation' was another ingenious and artistic trick; for 'tribe' connotes a small agglomeration of human beings, 'nation' a large one. Plenty of people, as I shall show later, are interested in the local or vocational politics that affect their daily lives. And they are not only interested in them; they are well qualified to handle these small problems successfully. But few, on the contrary, are interested in national and international politics; and fewer still are qualified to cope with the major problems of statesmanship. By using the word 'tribe', Mr Chesterton evoked the cosy and idyllic atmosphere of the Greek or mediaeval city-state, of the Indian wigwam and the palaeolithic cave. 'Nation' would have summoned up all the enormously complicated and uncomfortable realities of modern industrial life. Mr Chesterton is an artist in words; it is a pleasure to draw attention to his artistry). Men ought, I repeat, to take an interest in law-making. But in point of fact they seem, at ordinary times, to take very little interest. A considerable proportion of voters never vote at all. My morning paper informs me very opportunely that at the Brixton bye-election (27th June 1927) only 53 per cent. of the electorate voted. In this borough nearly half the men and women who ought to have been helping to rule the tribe were so little interested in the process that they could not trouble to walk to a polling booth. So much for the non-voters. And out of every hundred of those who do use their privilege at election time, how many take a consistent and intelligent interest in politics in the unexciting interval? If we compare the numbers of voters enrolled as members of the various political parties with the total number of voters on the registers, we shall be able to form some idea of the ratio of politically interested to politically uninterested people. It will be found that the uninterested are in an enormous majority. It is almost inevitable that this should be so, for it is a matter of common observation that few men, and vastly fewer women, are interested in things which do not immediately affect their daily lives. Whenever government becomes so intolerably bad that it seriously affects the interests of each individual, when it oppressively robs men of the comfort, the prosperity, the personal privileges to which they have been brought up to think

E 63

themselves entitled, people tend to take a passionate interest in law-making. The standard of governmental oppressiveness varies from age to age with the standard of living and the ideas of inherent rights and privileges current among the oppressed. The contemporary French peasant would revolt against any government which attempted to do a hundredth part of the things which were done as a matter of course under the *ancien régime*. His standard of living is so much higher than that of his ancestors, he takes for granted as natural and inalienable so many rights and privileges of which they never dreamed, that for him a government is oppressive when it acts in ways which his fathers would have regarded, not merely as not particularly oppressive, but even as actually humane. In different societies governments reach the oppression-point at different times; but when the point is reached the reaction, in the shape of intense political interest, is always the same. When the particular grievances which brought dissatisfaction to a head have been remedied, the sustained interest in politics dies down, and as long as the rulers govern in such a way that the ruled do not feel themselves adversely affected personally by their activities, so long as circumstances remain normally propitious (for political unrest may be aroused by accidents over which the rulers have no control, and for which they are in no way responsible), the interest will remain in abeyance.

Interest being proportionate to the distance of the object from the individual, we should naturally expect to find a generally keener interest in local than in national politics. The facts seem at first sight to disprove the general rule. For municipal elections rouse less excitement than general elections; the number of people who use their local vote is much smaller than the number of those who use their national vote. This seems paradoxical, but in fact is not. For to the inhabitants of a town the local politics need not necessarily be nearer, in the psychological sense, than the affairs of the nation as a whole. If the municipal administration is tolerably efficient, there is no reason why men and women should be in any way personally conscious of municipal politics.

Nor is there any artificial agency for creating the interest which is naturally lacking. For newspapers which are always clamorously urging their readers to take an interest in national politics have little or nothing to say about local politics. Much nearer than municipal politics, as distance is measured psychologically, are the politics of vocation. A man may live all his life in a town without ever once being made personally and intimately aware of its politics. But he can hardly fail to be aware of the politics of his trade or profession. Half, at least, of the hours of his waking life are passed at work, and the whole of his material interests are determined by it. National and municipal politics may easily, by reason of their psychological remoteness, be matters of indifference; but not vocational politics. The major vocational problems are also national and international problems. Feeling that these problems are close to him, the average man is interested in them, and to this extent is interested in law-making on the grand scale. The granting of a constitution to India was an act intrinsically quite as important as the withdrawal of the Coal Trade subsidy; but for every man interested in the first piece of statesmanship there were a hundred interested in the second. India is a long way off in space, and for those who have never been there it is more distant psychologically than the moon. The moon, at any rate, had a decided effect upon love-making and melancholy meditation; but there is no reason why India should ever touch us at all.

I have been at some pains to show that, whatever they theoretically ought to do, most men are not in fact much interested in politics which do not directly and obviously affect their everyday lives. This was necessary, because it is impossible to criticize a political ideal without knowing the reality to which it refers. For example, the ideal that men should share their possessions is one in which many people have enthusiastically believed. Judged by religious and transcendental-ethical criteria, it may be an excellent idea. The earliest Christians seem, for a short time at any rate, to have been practising communists. Covetousness and selfishness are vices. These facts are regarded by some people as valid reasons for believing in communism. Not, however, by politicians; for they are facts that tell us nothing about the political, as opposed to the religious and transcendental-ethical, values of the ideal. Its political value can only be assessed when we know how the majority of human beings feel about private property. If we observe that as a matter of fact most men and women are passionately interested in private property, we shall not regard the idea as politically very sound. And our conviction of its political unsoundness will be confirmed if we find that the practical applications of the ideal have not been successful. Mr Chesterton's democratic faith, that the making of laws must be left to ordinary men themselves, must be judged, in so far as it is a political ideal, in the same way. We must discover first, whether ordinary men are interested in making laws; and in the second place, whether their participation in the government of states has in fact been successful. If they are not interested in ruling the tribe, and if there their efforts to do so have not in practice 'worked', then we are justified in supposing that the ideal in which Mr Chesterton believes is not, politically speaking, a sound ideal.

POLITICAL DEMOCRACY IN PRACTICE

The first of these questions has already been answered. Ordinary men, we have seen, are not much interested in any political problems which do not immediately affect themselves. Let us consider, very briefly, the second question, which may be re-stated succinctly thus: Has political democracy worked, does it work now, and is it likely to go on working in the future? That the lot of ordinary men has been enormously ameliorated in the period during which political democracy has been in practice might seem, at a first glance, to constitute an unequivocally affirmative answer. But a little reflection is enough to convince one that it does not. Political democracy and the amelioration of the common lot are not connected in any necessary way. It is perfectly possible for an autocracy or an oligarchy to be humane, and for a democratically organized government to be oppressive. The common man's lot happens to have been improved during the democratic era, and the improvement has been to a great extent directly due to democracy. We may be duly grateful to democracy without allowing our gratitude to blind us to its defects, and without forgetting that the process of amelioration can be continued under other and politically more satisfactory systems. Not only can it be continued, but, as I shall try to show later, it must be continued— must, that is to say, if the existing system is to be succeeded by a more rational mode of government. The condition, alas, need not necessarily be fulfilled.

The defects of political democracy as a system of government are so obvious, and have so often been catalogued, that I need not do more than summarize them here. Political democracy has been blamed because it leads to inefficiency and weakness of rule, because it permits the least desirable men to obtain power, because it encourages corruption. The inefficiency and weakness of political democracy are most apparent in moments of crisis, when decisions have to be rapidly made and acted upon. To ascertain and tabulate the wishes of many millions of electors in a few hours is a physical impossibility. It follows, therefore, that in a crisis one of two things must happen: either the governors decide and present the accomplished fact of their decision to the electors—in which case the whole principle of political democracy will have been treated with the contempt which in critical circumstances it deserves; or else the people are consulted and time is lost, with often fatal consequences. During the War all the belligerents adopted the first course. Political democracy was everywhere temporarily abolished. A system of government which requires to be abolished every time a danger presents itself can hardly be described as a perfect system.

The chronic, as opposed to the occasional, weakness of a democratic system of government seems to be proportionate to the degree of its democratization. The most powerful and stable democratic states are those in which the principles of democracy have been least logically and consistently applied. The weakest are the most democratic. Thus a parliament elected under a scheme of proportional representation is a truly democratic parliament. But it is also, in most cases, an instrument not of rule but of anarchy. Proportional representation guarantees that all shades of opinion shall be represented in the assembly. It is the ideal of democracy fulfilled. Unfortunately the multiplication of small groups within the parliament makes the formation of a stable and powerful government impossible. In proportionally elected assemblies governments must generally rely on a composite majority. They have to buy the support of small groups with the more or less corrupt distribution of favours, and as they can never give enough, they are liable to be defeated at any moment. Proportional representation in Italy led through anarchy to fascism. It has caused great practical difficulties in Belgium, and threatens now to do the same in Ireland. Stable democratic governments are found in countries where minorities, however large, are unrepresented, and where no candidate who does not belong to one of the great parties has the slightest chance of being elected. Parliaments in such countries are not in the least representative of the people. They are thoroughly undemocratic. But they possess one great merit which makes up for all their defects: they can form governments strong enough to govern.

Government of whatever kind is superior to anarchy. We must be thankful for a system which gives us stable government, even when, as happens only too frequently in democratic countries, the men who direct the government are charlatans and rogues. Fate has afflicted the nations with many disastrous monarchs. Hereditary tyrants have often been born imbeciles and bred up to be spendthrifts or criminals. We may feel sincerely sorry for people who through no fault of their own have found themselves saddled with a Nero, a King John, a Kaiser William the Second. But for those who of their own free will elect a Bottomley as their parliamentary representative, a Big Bill Thompson as their mayor (not once, but, in spite of the first disastrous experience, a second time), one can feel less sympathy.

The most monstrous rulers have certainly been hereditary despots, not the elected representatives of the people. But we must remember that the history of democracy has been a short one compared with that of despotism. In a century and a half even autocracy could produce few first-rate tyrants. Moreover, the democratic ruler comes to power relatively later in life, and so has had less chances of being corrupt. (The facility with which youths can be corrupted by the premature possession of power or wealth constitutes one of the main arguments against the hereditary principle in government.) It would be surprising if democracy had produced a crop of Neros; for Neros must be made as well as born, and democracy gives little scope for their manufacture. But though democracy can boast no Nero—only a Robespierre or two and some Djerzhinskys—it has produced a whole Newgate Calendar of lesser ruffians. The history of corruption in all democratic countries, particularly America, is full of heroes. And as for the charlatans and the criminal incompetents—their name is all but legion. This is only to be expected, since the talents required to win public favour are quite different from those which a ruler ought to possess. Demagogues succeed for the same reason as confidence tricksters —because they have a gift of the gab, charm, and an intuitive knowledge of human nature, because their personality is magnetic, and their manner open and affable. Men and women are so suggestible, so easily gulled, that a talented swindler can always be certain of making a handsome living. How much more certain of success is a demagogue! For demagogues do not ask their victims to give them a wad of banknotes; they only ask for votes. You can buy things with banknotes, voting papers are worth nothing. Every one is prepared to be generous with his vote. The best democratic leaders have either, by a coincidence, possessed both the swindler's and the statesman's talents, or else have risen to power by undemocratic means. Disraeli was a great political genius who happened also to be a great demagogue. Lord Salisbury was also an excellent statesman; but he would never have become prime minister in a democratically organized country if he had not been Robert Arthur Talbot Gascoyne-Cecil and a Third Marquess.

Demagogues are not the only or even the most efficient exploiters of human suggestibility. The newspaper proprietors have carried the art of the confidence trickster to a yet higher pitch. The spread of elementary education has been accompanied by a great increase in the influence of the press. Who reads may run—in the same direction as his newspaper. This is a fact of which the rich were not slow to take advantage. Practically speaking, the whole English press is now in the hands of four or five rich men. Plutocratic oligarchs, they aspire to rule, under cover of democratic institutions, impersonally and without responsibility. To exploit democracy, they have seen, is easier and more profitable than to oppose it. Let the many vote, but as the opulent few who won the newspapers tell them. The many obey —generally, but not always. Elections may be won, as was demonstrated by the Liberals in 1906, by the Labour Party in 1923, in the teeth of an almost unanimously hostile press. The newspaper proprietors will not rule undisputedly until they have discovered in what circumstances men assent, and in what others they respond to suggestion by deliberate contradiction. They have already realized (what schoolmasters have discovered long ago) that indirect suggestion is less liable to arouse contradiction than direct. Doctored news convinces much more effectually than many dogmatic leading articles. But the science of journalistic confidence trickery is still in its infancy. A time will doubtless come when the propagandist methods of contemporary newspaper owners will seem barbarically crude and inept.

The third main objection to political democracy is that it encourages corruption. The evidence for democratic corruption is written so large over recent American and European history that it is unnecessary for me to catalogue specific instances. I shall confine myself to a few general reflections. Men are afflicted with the original sin of their anti-social instincts, which remain more or less uniform throughout the ages. The tendency towards corruption is implanted in human nature from the first.

Some men have strength enough to resist the tendency, others have not. There has been corruption under every system of government. Corruption under the democratic system is not worse, in the individual cases, than corruption under autocracy. There is merely more of it, for the simple reason that where government is popular, more people have an opportunity for acting corruptly at the expense of the state than in countries where government is autocratic. In autocratically organized states the loot of government is shared among a few. In democratic states there are many more claimants, who can only be satisfied with a much greater total quantity of loot than was necessary to satisfy the aristocratic few. Experience has shown that democratic government is generally much more expensive than government by the few.

THE IDEAL IN THE LIGHT OF REALITY

It is now time to reconsider Mr Chesterton's ideal. Ordinary men, he says, ought to take part in government. But in fact they are not much interested in law-making, while the systems of government which invite them to take part in ruling the tribe are far from satisfactory. Can we, in the light of these facts, go on believing in Mr Chesterton's ideal? Mr Chesterton has tried to anticipate criticism by saying that ordinary men ought to govern, even though they do it badly. It was in the same spirit that a Filipino leader recently declared that home rule for the Philippines was desirable, even though it meant 'making hell' of the islands. Once more we can only appeal to the historical reality. Have men in fact enjoyed being governed badly, even when they themselves took part in the government? Have they felt comfortable in hell, even when the hell was of their own making? The answer, surely, is that they have not. Whenever government, even self-government, has reached a certain stage of inefficiency, men have invariably welcomed even a despot, provided that he could give them law and order. Falling in love, says Mr Chesterton, is more poetical than dropping into poetry, and governing is, or ought to be, like falling in love. But if one wants to read poetry, one would rather read the poetry of Keats than that of an ordinary love-sick young man. Even the ordinary young man himself, however much he enjoys falling in love, prefers Keats's poetry to his own. It is the same with government. Helping to rule the tribe may be a very poetical act in itself (though few people seem to find it so); but the act has results, and the results may be as bad, in their practical way, as the love-sick young man's verses. History shows that men prefer the political harmonies of the statesman of genius to their own ineffectual or disastrous efforts at ruling. The finished and perfected poetry of good rule seems to them more valuable than the very indifferently poetical act of helping to govern badly.

The passionate quality of Mr Chesterton's faith in political democracy seems to be explained by the fact that he can see no alternative to inefficient government by the people except corrupt government by the rich. I share his mistrust of the rich, and believe so firmly in the truth of that distressing saying about the camel and the needle's eye that I should feel exceedingly uncomfortable if some capricious fate were suddenly to make me a millionaire. If plutocracy were indeed the only alternative to inefficient democracy, I should certainly be a good deal less anxious to change the existing state of affairs. But wealth is not the only source of power, nor mens' only qualification to rule. There is also, after all, intelligence. Mr Chesterton finds something poetical about the idea of the ordinary man governing badly; he approves of the system which invites him to do his worst with the ship of state. Personally I find the idea of being governed well (I myself lack all capacity or ambition to govern) much more poetical; and I should be in favour of any system which secured intelligent men with a talent for government to do the ruling.

ARISTOCRACY

The creation and maintenance of a ruling aristocracy of mind would not in any degree endanger the cause of humanitarianism. Indeed it would be necessary, in an aristocratically governed state, to carry humanitarianism much further than it has been carried in the democratic state. In a country where it is a principle that the naturally best men should be at the top, careers must be wide open to the talents, and the material conditions of life must be, for all, the most propitious that can be designed. For the naturally best man is so rare that one cannot afford to let him be stunted by an unfavourable environment, or kept down by lack of opportunity. A state that is aristocratic in the etymological sense of the term—a state, that is to say, which is ruled by the best of its citizens—must be socially much more democratic than any state which we know at present. In the contemporary democratic state it is possible for the worst to govern and for the best, if they happen to be born in unfavourable surroundings, to be distorted by disease and hunger, handicapped mentally by inadequate education, and wasted throughout an entire lifetime on unsuitable work. True aristocracy can only exist where there are no hereditary advantages other than those of talent, and where the rich cannot claim to rule on the mere ground that they are rich. It is obviously very unlikely that any of those now living will ever see a genuinely aristocratic state. Indeed, the genuinely aristocratic state may be an actually unrealizable ideal. But it is at least an unrealizable ideal which may be approached in practice without involving in insoluble difficulties those who try to apply it. For it is an ideal which takes into account the unalterable realities of human nature. There are other finally unrealizable ideals which do not take the facts of life into consideration, and which consequently plunge into immediate difficulties all who act in accordance with them. Mr Chesterton's democratic ideal is an ideal of the second kind. Finally unrealizable, it also leads to immediate trouble when applied in practice. The aristocratic ideal may be equally unrealizable (though even this is not certain); but since it is based on an acceptance of the facts, its gradual application to politics cannot be attended by serious difficulties.

The ideal of aristocracy is already acted upon in so many spheres of our social life that its application to all the spheres, including that of government, ought not to be a matter of insuperable difficulty. It is the unfamiliar that men dislike; the already familiar idea can be developed without arousing any violent terror or rage. The aristocratic ideal—the ideal that the naturally best men should be at the top—is already extremely familiar. In commerce and industry promotion is regarded as the reward of superior capacity. The higher posts are still, it is true, mainly filled by men with hereditary or financial influence. But as economic pressure increases, influential incompetence tends to be squeezed out, while the men with ability are forced up from below to take their places. In the lower ranks influence counts less and the ideal of aristocracy is consistently acted upon. The professions are genuinely aristocratic institutions. Doctors and lawyers, engineers and architects, are only permitted to practise if they have shown themselves competent to pass a test of ability. Tests no less stringent are applied to candidates for official posts under the government. This last fact is particularly significant. Even in the most democratic countries civil servants are expected to show some symptom of exceptional ability. They must be mentally aristocratic—to the extent, at any rate, of being able to pass an examination. (That the existing system of examinations excludes some of the best men is notorious; but that it also excludes most of the worst is no less indubitable. This is a matter to which I shall return at a later stage.)

Our modern governments, then, are anomalous. On their administrative side they are definitely aristocratic. Nobody may be a civil servant who has not passed a test of capacity. But any one may vote provided he is twenty-one years old. (In France it has been decided in a court of law that certified idiots have a right to vote.) And any one who is not actually a criminal may stand for parliament, and so be qualified to become a cabinet minister. This is a manifestly absurd state of affairs. The men who administer the laws have to give proof of ability and know-ledge: the men who make the laws need give proof of nothing at all except the confidence trickster's ability to talk persuasively, or, lacking that, the possession of money or some sort of influence. And yet to make the laws is at least as difficult as to administer them. Indeed, it is much more difficult; for while the administrator deals with only one kind of law referring to one class of social activities, the law-maker has to consider laws on every subject, and is responsible for all the policies, national and international, industrial, commercial, economic, of a whole country. A man who proposes to become a first-class clerk in a government department is required to prove himself intelligent and well educated. How much more intelligent, how much better educated, should be the member of parliament who makes the laws that are administered, not in one, but in all the departments! In actual fact, however, an average member of parliament is less intelligent and incomparably worse educated than the average higher-grade civil servant. This, I know, is a sweeping general-ization: but any one who has a wide acquaintance among both classes of men will find the truth of it confirmed by daily observation. I have met members of parliament who, whatever their wealth or their powers of tub-thumping might have been, would quite certainly have been unable to enter even the lower grades of the civil service or to work their way in commerce above the rank of copying-clerk.

It would be possible, without making any radical changes in the existing system, to improve the quality of the legislative assembly, simply by demanding from the legislator the same proofs of competence as are demanded from every administrator. If nobody were allowed to stand for parliament who had not shown himself at least capable of entering the higher grades of the civil service, parliament would automatically be purged of many of its worst incompetents and charlatans. It is possible that if this test were imposed a few men of real merit might be excluded, but their loss would be compensated by the exclusion of so many merely talkative and merely rich or influential people, so many ignorant quacks and rogues. If at the same time the right to vote were made contingent on the ability to pass a fairly stiff intelligence test—if nobody were allowed to partici-pate in the government of the country who was not mentally at least fifteen years old—it is probable that the influence of demagogues and newspapers would be considerably reduced. Adults are more judicious, less easily suggestible, than children.

That only mental grown-ups should vote, and that nobody should be allowed to make laws who is not at least as intelligent and well informed as the men who administer them—these are political principles which ordinary common sense must approve. Only the most mystically fervent democrats, who regard voting as a kind of religious act, and who hear the voice of God in that of the People, can have any reason to desire to perpetuate a system whereby confidence tricksters, rich men, and quacks may be given power by the votes of an electorate composed in a great part of mental Peter Pans, whose childishness renders them peculiarly susceptible to the blandishments of demagogues and the tirelessly repeated suggestions of the rich men's newspapers. The principle which makes right and privileges dependent on capacity is so well established in almost every sphere of human activity that the idea of applying it to the organization of government cannot be regarded as strange and revolutionary. Not merely common sense, but even social tradition, can be enlisted on the side of reforms that seek to establish government by grown-ups and men of tested ability for the present chaotic and haphazard system.

These simple reforms would not, it is obvious, transform political democracy at one stroke into aristocracy. They would constitute at most a first step in the right direction—towards government by those best fitted to govern. As things are at present, we do not even make an effort to have ourselves ruled by the most fit; we simply leave the whole matter to chance. Sometimes a few good men appear among the riff-raff of lawmakers, sometimes the riff-raff is unadulterated. Fate chooses; we do not. But even if we ardently desired to select the best men, we should not know how to make the selection with anything like accuracy or certainty. The existing tests of ability are certainly better than nothing; but they are still crude and inadequate.

COMFORT

From *Proper Studies* (1927)

FRENCH hotel-keepers call it *Le confort moderne*, and they are right. For comfort is a thing of recent growth, younger than steam, a child when telegraphy was born, only a generation older than radio. The invention of the means of being comfortable and the pursuit of comfort as a desirable end—one of the most desirable that human beings can propose to themselves—are modern phenomena, unparalleled in history since the time of the Romans. Like all phenomena with which we are extremely familiar, we take them for granted, as a fish takes the water in which it lives, not realizing the oddity and novelty of them, not bothering to consider their significance. The padded chair, the well-sprung bed, the sofa, central heating, and the regular hot bath—these and a host of other comforts enter into the daily lives of even the most moderately prosperous of the Anglo-Saxon bourgeoisie. Three hundred years ago they were unknown to the greatest kings. This is a curious fact which deserves to be examined and analysed.

The first thing that strikes one about the discomfort in which our ancestors lived is that it was mainly voluntary. Some of the apparatus of modern comfort is of purely modern invention; people could not put rubber tyres on their carriages before the discovery of South America and the rubber plant. But for the most part there is nothing new about the material basis of our comfort. Men could have made sofas and smoking-room chairs, could have installed bathrooms and central heating and sanitary plumbing any time during the last three or four thousand years. And as a matter of fact, at certain periods they did indulge themselves in these comforts. Two thousand years before Christ, the inhabitants of Cnossos were familiar with sanitary plumbing.

The Romans had invented an elaborate system of hot-air heating, and the bathing facilities in a smart Roman villa were luxurious and complete beyond the dreams of the modern man. There were sweating-rooms, massage-rooms, cold plunges, tepid drying-rooms with (if we may believe Sidonius Apollinaris) improper frescoes on the walls and comfortable couches where you could lie and get dry and talk to your friends. As for the public baths they were almost inconceivably luxurious. 'To such a height of luxury have we reached', said Seneca, 'that we are dissatisfied if, in our baths, we do not tread on gems.' The size and completeness of the thermae was proportionable to their splendour. A single room of the baths of Diocletian has been transformed into a large church.

It would be possible to adduce many other examples showing what could be done with the limited means at our ancestors' disposal in the way of making life comfortable. They show sufficiently clearly that if the men of the Middle Ages and early modern epoch lived in filth and discomfort, it was not for any lack or ability to change their mode of life; it was because they chose to live in this way, because filth and discomfort fitted in with their principles and prejudices, political, moral, and religious.

COMFORT AND THE SPIRITUAL LIFE

What have comfort and cleanliness to do with politics, morals, and religion? At a first glance one would say that there was and could be no causal connection between armchairs and democracies, sofas and the relaxation of the family system, hot baths and the decay of Christian orthodoxy. But look more closely and you will discover that there exists the closest connection between the recent growth of comfort and the recent history of ideas. I hope in this essay to make that connection manifest, to show why it was not possible (not materially, but psychologically impossible) for the Italian princes of the quattrocento, for the Elizabethan, even for Louis XIV to live in what the Romans would have called common cleanliness and decency, or enjoy what would be to us indispensable comforts.

Let us begin with the consideration of armchairs and central heating. These, I propose to show, only became possible with the breakdown of monarchical and feudal power and the decay of the old family and social hierarchies. Smoking-room chairs and sofas exist to be lolled in. In a well-made modern armchair you cannot do anything but loll. Now, lolling is neither dignified nor respectful. When we wish to appear impressive, when we have to administer, a rebuke to an inferior we do not lie in a deep chair with our feet on the mantelpiece; we sit up and try to look majestical. Similarly, when we wish to be polite to a lady or show respect to the old or eminent, we cease to loll; we stand, or at least we straighten ourselves up. Now, in the past human society was a hierarchy in which every man was always engaged in being impressive towards his inferiors or respectful to those above him. Lolling in such societies was utterly impossible. It was as much out of the question for Louis XIV to loll in the presence of his courtiers as it was for them to loll in the presence of their king. It was only when he attended a session of the Parlement that the King of France ever lolled in public. On these occasions he reclined in the Bed of Justice, while princes sat, the great officers of the crown stood, and the smaller fry knelt. Comfort was proclaimed as the appanage of royalty. Only the king might stretch his legs. We may feel sure, however, that he stretched them in a very majestic manner. The lolling was purely ceremonial and accompanied by no loss of dignity. At ordinary times the king was seated, it is true, but seated in a dignified and upright position; the appearance of majesty had to be kept up. (For, after all, majesty is mainly a question of majestical appearance.) The courtiers, meanwhile, kept up the appearances of deference, either standing, or else, if their rank was very high and their blood peculiarly blue, sitting, even in the royal presence, on stools. What was true of the king's court was true of the nobleman's household; and the squire was to his dependants, the merchant was to his apprentices and servants, what the monarch was to his courtiers. In all cases the superior had to express his superiority by being dignified, the inferior his inferiority by being deferential; there could be no lolling. Even in the intimacies of family life it was the same; the parents ruled like popes and princes, by divine right; the children were their subjects. Our fathers took the fifth commandment very seriously —how seriously may be judged from the fact that during the great Calvin's theocratic rule of Geneva a child was publicly decapitated for having ventured to strike its parents. Lolling on the part of children, though not perhaps a capital offence, would have been regarded as an act of the grossest disrespect, punishable by much flagellation, starving, and confinement. For a slighter insult—neglect to touch his cap—Vespasiano Gonzaga kicked his only son to death; one shudders to think what he might have been provoked to do if the boy had lolled. If the children might not loll in the presence of their parents, neither might the parents loll in the presence of their children, for fear of demeaning themselves in the eyes of those whose duty it was to honour them. Thus we see that in the European society of two or three hundred years ago it was impossible for any one—from the Holy Roman Emperor and the King of France down to the poorest beggar, from the bearded patriarch to the baby—to loll in the presence of any one else. Old furniture reflects the physical habits of the hierarchical society for which it was made. It was in the power of mediaeval and renaissance craftsmen to create armchairs and sofas that might have rivalled in comfort those of today. But society being what, in fact, it was, they did nothing of the kind. It was not, indeed, until the sixteenth century that chairs became at all common. Before that time a chair was a symbol of authority. Committee-men now loll, Members of Parliament are comfortably seated, but authority still belongs to a Chairman, still issues from a symbolical Chair. In the Middle Ages only the great had chairs. When a great man travelled, he took his chair with him, so that he might never be seen detached from the outward and visible sign of his authority. To this day the Throne no less than the Crown is the symbol of royalty. In mediaeval times the vulgar sat, whenever it was permissible for them to sit, on benches, stools, and settles. With the rise, during the Renaissance period, of a rich and independent bourgeoisie, chairs began to be more freely used. Those who could afford chairs sat in them, but sat with dignity and discomfort; for the chairs of the sixteenth century were still very throne-like, and imposed upon those who sat in them a painfully majestic attitude. It was only in the eighteenth century, when the old hierarchies were seriously breaking up, that furniture began to be comfortable. And even then there was no real lolling. Armchairs and sofas on which men (and, later, women) might indecorously sprawl, were not made until democracy was firmly established, the middle classes enlarged to gigantic proportions, good manners lost from out of the world, women emancipated, and family restraints dissolved.

CENTRAL HEATING AND THE FEUDAL SYSTEM

Another essential component of modern comfort—the adequate heating of houses—was made impossible, at least for the great ones of the earth, by the political structure of ancient societies. Plebeians were more fortunate in this respect than nobles. Living in small houses, they were able to keep warm. But the nobleman, the prince, the king, and the cardinal inhabited palaces of a grandeur corresponding with their social position. In order to prove that they were greater than other men, they had to live in surroundings considerably more than life-size. They received their guests in vast halls like roller-skating rinks; they marched in solemn processions along galleries as long and as draughty as Alpine tunnels, up and down triumphal staircases that looked like the cataracts of the Nile frozen into marble. Being what he was, a great man in those days had to spend a great deal of his time in performing solemn symbolical charades and pompous ballets—performances which required a lot of room to accommodate the numerous actors and spectators. This explains the enormous dimensions of royal and princely palaces, even of the houses of ordinary landed gentlemen. They owed it to their position to live, as though they were giants, in rooms a hundred feet long and thirty high. How splendid, how magnificent! But oh, how bleak! In our days the self-made great are not expected to keep up their position in the splendid style of those who were great by divine right. Sacrificing grandiosity to comfort, they live in rooms small enough to be heated. (And so, when they were off duty, did the great in the past; most old palaces contain a series of tiny apartments to which their owners retired when the charades of state were over. But the charades were long-drawn affairs, and the unhappy princes of old days had to spend a great deal of time being magnificent in icy audience-chambers and among the whistling draughts of interminable galleries.) Driving in the environs of Chicago, I was shown the house of a man who was reputed to be one of the richest and most influential of the city. It was a medium-sized house of perhaps fifteen to twenty smallish rooms. I looked at it in astonishment, thinking of the vast palaces in which I myself have lived in Italy (for considerably less rent than one would have to pay for garaging a Ford in Chicago). I remembered the rows of bedrooms as big as ordinary ballrooms, the drawing-rooms like railway-stations, the staircase on which you could drive a couple of limousines abreast. Noble *palazzi*, where one has room to feel oneself a superman! But remembering also those terrible winds that blow in February from the Apennines, I was inclined to think that the rich man of Chicago had done well in sacrificing the magnificences on which his counterpart in another age and country would have spent his riches.

BATHS AND MORALS

It is to the decay of monarchy, aristocracy, and ancient social hierarchy that we owe the two components of modern comfort hitherto discussed; the third great component—the bath—must, I think, be attributed, at any rate in part, to the decay of Christian morals. There are still on the continent of Europe, and for all I know, elsewhere, convent schools in which young ladies are brought up to believe that human bodies are objects of so impure and obscene a character that it is sinful for them to see, not merely other people's nakedness, but even their own. Baths, when they are permitted to take them (every alternate Saturday) must be taken in a chemise descending well below the knees. And they are even taught a special technique of dressing which guarantees them from catching so much as a glimpse of their own skin. These schools are now, happily, exceptional, but there was a time, not so long ago, when they were the rule. Theirs is the great Christian ascetic tradition which has flowed on in majestic continuity from the time of St. Anthony and the unwashed, underfed, sex-starved monks of the Thebaid, through the centuries, almost to the present day. It is to the weakening of that tradition that women at any rate owe the luxury of frequent bathing.

The early Christians were by no means enthusiastic bathers; but it is fair to point out that Christian ascetic tradition has not at all times been hostile to baths as such. That the Early Fathers should have found the promiscuity of Roman bathing shocking is only natural. But the more moderate of them were prepared to allow a limited amount of washing, provided that the business was done with decency. The final decay of the great Roman baths was as much due to the destructiveness of the Barbarians as to Christian ascetic objections. During the Ages of Faith there was actually a revival of bathing. The Crusaders came back from the East, bringing with them the oriental vapour bath, which seems to have had a considerable popularity all over Europe. For reasons which it is difficult to understand, its popularity gradually waned, and the men and women of the late sixteenth and early seventeenth centuries seem to have been almost as dirty as their barbarous ancestors. Medical theory and court fashions may have had something to do with these fluctuations.

The ascetic tradition was always strongest where women were concerned. The Goncourts record in their diary the opinion, which seems to have been current in respectable circles during the Second Empire, that female immodesty and immorality had increased with the growth of the bath habit. 'Girls should wash less', was the obvious corollary. Young ladies who enjoy their bath owe a debt of gratitude to Voltaire for his mockeries, to the nineteenth-century scientists for their materialism. If these men had never lived to undermine the convent school tradition, our girls might still be as modest and as dirty as their ancestresses.

COMFORT AND MEDICINE

It is, however, to the doctors that bath-lovers owe their greatest debt. The discovery of microbic infection has put a premium on cleanliness. We wash now with religious fervour, like the Hindus. Our baths have become something like magic rites to protect us from the powers of evil, embodied in the dirt-loving germ. We may venture to prophesy that this medical religion will go still further in undermining the Christian ascetic tradition. Since the discovery of the beneficial effects of sunlight, too much clothing has become, medically speaking, a sin. Immodesty is now a virtue. It is quite likely that the doctors, whose prestige among us is almost equal to that of the medicine men among their savages, will have us stark naked before very long. That will be the last stage in the process of making clothes more comfortable. It is a process which has been going on for some time—first among men, later among women—and among its determining causes are the decay of hierarchic formalism and of Christian morality. In his lively little pamphlet describing Gladstone's visit to Oxford shortly before his death, Mr Fletcher has recorded the Grand Old Man's comments on the dress of the undergraduates. Mr Gladstone, it appears, was distressed by the informality and the cheapness of the students' clothes. In his day, he said, young men went about with a hundred pounds worth of clothes and jewellery on their persons, and every self-respecting youth had at least one pair of trousers in which he never sat down for fear of spoiling its shape. Mr Gladstone visited Oxford at a time when undergraduates still wore very high starched collars and bowler hats. One wonders what he would have said of the open shirts, the gaudily coloured sweaters, the loose flannel trousers of the present generation. Dignified appearances have never been less assiduously kept up than they are at present; informality has reached an unprecedented pitch. On all but the most solemn occasions a man, whatever his rank or position, may wear what he finds comfortable.

The obstacles in the way of women's comforts were moral as well as political. Women were compelled not merely to keep up social appearances, but also to conform to a tradition of Christian ascetic morality. Long after men had abandoned their uncomfortable formal clothes, women were still submitting to extraordinary inconveniences in the name of modesty. It was the war which liberated them from their bondage. When women began to do war work, they found that the traditional modesty in dress was not compatible with efficiency. They preferred to be efficient. Having discovered the advantages of immodesty, they have remained immodest ever since, to the great improvement of their health and increase of their personal comfort. Modern fashions are the most comfortable that women have ever worn. Even the ancient Greeks were probably less comfortable. Their under-tunic, it is true, was as rational a garment as you could wish for; but their outer robe was simply a piece of stuff wound round the body like an Indian *sari*, and fastened with safety-pins. No woman whose appearance depended on safety-pins can ever have felt really comfortable.

COMFORT AS AN END IN ITSELF

Made possible by changes in the traditional philosophy of life, comfort is now one of the causes of its own further spread. For comfort has now become a physical habit, a fashion, an ideal to be pursued for its own sake. The more comfort is brought into the world, the more it is likely to be valued. To those who have known comfort, discomfort is a real torture. And the fashion which now decrees the worship of comfort is quite as imperious as any other fashion. Moreover, enormous material interests are bound up with the supply of the means of comfort. The manufacturers of furniture, of heating apparatus, of plumbing fixtures, cannot afford to let the love of comfort die. In modern advertisement they have means for compelling it to live and grow.

Having now briefly traced the spiritual origins of modern comfort, I must say a few words about its effects. One can never have something for nothing, and the achievement of comfort has been accompanied by a compensating loss of other equally, or perhaps more, valuable things. A man of means who builds a house today is in general concerned primarily with the comfort of his future residence. He will spend a great deal of money (for comfort is very expensive: In America they talk of giving away the house with the plumbing) on bathrooms, heating apparatus, padded furnishings, and the like; and having spent it, he will regard his house as perfect. His counterpart in an earlier age would have been primarily concerned with the impressiveness and magnificence of his dwelling—with beauty, in a word, rather than comfort. The money our contemporary would spend on baths and central heating would have been spent in the past on marble staircases, a grand façade, frescoes, huge suites of gilded rooms, pictures, statues. Sixteenth-century popes lived in a discomfort that a modern bank manager would consider unbearable; but they had Raphael's frescoes, they had the Sistine chapel, they had their galleries of ancient sculpture. Must we pity them for the absence from the Vatican of bathrooms, central heating, and smoking-room chairs? I am inclined to think that our present passion for comfort is a little exaggerated. Though I personally enjoy comfort, I have lived very happily in houses devoid of almost everything that Anglo-Saxons deem indispensable. Orientals and even South Europeans, who know not comfort and live very much as our ancestors lived centuries ago, seem to get on very well without our elaborate and costly apparatus of padded luxury. I am old-fashioned enough to believe in higher and lower things, and can see no point in material progress except in so far as it subserves thought. I like labour-saving devices, because they economize time and energy which may be devoted to mental labour. (But then I enjoy mental labour; there are plenty of people who detest it, and who feel as much enthusiasm for thought-saving devices as for automatic dishwashers and sewing-machines.) I like rapid and easy transport, because by enlarging the world in which men can live it enlarges their minds. Comfort for me has a similar justification: it facilitates mental life. Discomfort handicaps thought; it is difficult when the body is cold and aching to use the mind. Comfort is a means to an end. The modern world seems to regard it as an end in itself, an absolute good. One day, perhaps, the earth will have been turned into one vast feather-bed, with man's body dozing on top of it and his mind underneath, like Desdemona, smothered.

REVOLUTIONS

From *Do What You Will* (1929)

'THE Proletariat.' It was Karl Marx who enriched the dead and ugly gibbering of politicians and journalists and Thoughtful People (the gibbering which in certain circles is beautifully called 'the language of modern ideology') with the word. 'The Proletariat.' For Marx those five syllables connoted something extremely unpleasant, something very discreditable to humanity at large and the bourgeoisie in particular. Pronouncing them, he thought of life in the English manufacturing towns in the first half of the nineteenth century. He thought of children working a two-hundred-and-sixteen-hour week for a shilling. Of women being used, instead of the more costly horse, in pulling trucks of coal along the galleries of mines. Of men performing endless tasks in filthy, degrading, and unwholesome surroundings in order to earn enough for themselves and their families just not to starve on. He thought of all the iniquitous things that had been done in the name of Progress and National Prosperity. Of all the atrocious wickedness which piously Christian ladies and gentlemen complacently accepted and even personally participated in, because they were supposed to be inevitable, like sunrise and sunset, because they were supposed to happen in accordance with the changeless, the positively divine, laws of Political Economy.

The wage-slaves of the early and middle nineteenth century were treated a good deal worse than most of the chattel slaves of antiquity and modern times. Naturally; for a chattel slave was a valuable possession, and nobody wantonly destroys valuable possessions. It was only when conquest had made slaves enormously plentiful and cheap that the owner class permitted itself to be extravagant with its labour resources. Thus, the Spaniards wiped out the whole of the aboriginal population of the West Indies in a few generations. The average life of an Indian slave in a mine was about a year. When he had been worked to death, the mine-owner bought another slave, for practically nothing. Slaves were a natural product of the soil, which the Spaniards felt themselves at liberty to waste, as the Americans now feel themselves at liberty to waste petroleum. But in normal times, when the supply of slaves was limited, owners were more careful of their possessions. The slave was then treated with at least as much consideration as a mule or a donkey. Nineteenth-century industrialists were in the position of conquerors having a suddenly dilated supply of slave labour on which to draw. Machinery had increased production, hitherto empty lands were supplying cheap food, while imported nitrates were increasing the home supply. It was therefore possible for the population to increase, and, when it is possible for the population to increase, it generally does increase, rapidly at first, and then, as a certain density is approached, with diminishing acceleration. The industrials of last century were living at the time of the population's most rapid increase. There was an endless supply of slaves. They could afford to be extravagant; and, anaesthetizing their consciences with the consoling thought that it was all in accordance with those Iron Laws that were so popular in scientific circles at the period, and trusting with truly Christian faith that the wage-slaves would get their compensation in a Better World, they *were* extravagant—with a vengeance! Wage-slaves were worked to death at high speed; but there were always new ones coming in to take their places, fairly begging the capitalists to work *them* to death too. The efficiency of these slaves while being worked to death on starvation wages was, of course, very low; but there were so many of them, and they cost so little, that the owners could rely on quantity to make up for any defect in quality.

Such was the position in the industrial world when Marx wrote his celebrated and almost universally unread work. The Proletariat, as he knew it, was exploited and victimized as only, in the slave-holding past, the conquered had been exploited and victimized. Marx's whole theory of contemporary history and

SELECTED ESSAYS OF ALDOUS HUXLEY

future industrial development depended on the continual existence of precisely that particular Proletariat with which he was familiar. He did not foresee the possibility of that Proletariat ceasing to exist. For him it was to be for ever and inevitably victimized and exploited—that is, until revolution had founded the communist State.

The facts have proved him wrong. The Proletariat as he knew it had ceased—or, if that is too sweeping a statement, is ceasing —to exist in America and, to a less extent, industrialized Europe. The higher the degree of industrial development and material civilization (which is not at all the same thing, incidentally, as civilization *tout court*), the more complete has been the transformation of the Proletariat. In the most fully industrialized countries the Proletariat is no longer abject; it is prosperous, its way of life approximates to that of the bourgeoisie. No longer the victim, it is actually, in some places, coming to be the victimizer.

The causes of this change are many and diverse. In the depths of the human soul lies something which we rationalize as a demand for justice. It is an obscure perception of the necessity for balance in the affairs of life; we are conscious of it as a passion for equity, a hungering after righteousness. An obvious lack of balance in the outside world outrages this feeling for equity within us, gradually and cumulatively outrages it, until we are driven to react, often extravagantly, against the forces of disequilibrium. Just as the aristocratic power-holders of eighteenth-century France were driven, by their outraged sentiment of equity, to preach humanitarianism and equality, to give away their hereditary privileges and yield without a struggle to the demands of the revolutionaries, so the industrial-bourgeois power-holders of the nineteenth century passed laws to restrain their own cupidity, handed over more and more of their power to the Proletariat they had so outrageously oppressed, and even, in individual cases, took a strange masochistic pleasure in sacrificing themselves to the victims, serving the servants and being humiliated by the oppressed. If they had chosen to use their power ruthlessly, they could have gone on exploiting the wage-slaves as they exploited them in the earlier part of the century. But they simply could not make such a choice; for the unbalanced world of the early industrial epoch was felt by the deepest self as an outrage. Hence, in the later nineteenth century, that 'craven fear of being great' which afflicted and still afflicts the class of masters. Here then is one cause of the change. It is a cause which historical materialists, who deal not with real human beings but with abstract 'Economic Men', do not consider. It is none the less potent. In the world where historical materialists are at home, there were also good store of causes. Organization of the Proletariat. Revolutionary propaganda culminating in more or less revolutionary violence. And, above all, the momentous discovery that it pays the capitalist to have a prosperous Proletariat about him. It pays him to pay well, because those who are paid well buy well, particularly when hypnotized by the incessant suggestions of modern advertising. The policy of modern capitalism is to teach the Proletariat to be wasteful, to organize and facilitate its extravagance, and at the same time to make that extravagance possible by paying high wages in return for high production. The newly enriched Proletariat is suggested into spending what it earns, and even into mortgaging its future earnings in the purchase of objects which the advertisers persuasively affirm to be necessaries or at least indispensable luxuries. The money circulates and the prosperity of the modern industrial state is assured—until such time, at any rate, as the now extravagantly squandered resources of the planet begin to run low. But this eventuality is still, by the standards of an individual life, though not by those of history and infinitely less by those of geology, remote.

Meanwhile, what is happening, what is likely to happen in the future, to Karl Marx's Proletariat? Briefly, this is happening. It is becoming a branch of the bourgeoisie—a bourgeoisie that happens to work in factories and not in offices; a bourgeoisie with oily instead of inky fingers. Out of working hours the way of life of these two branches of the modern bourgeoisie is the same. Inevitably, since they earn the same wages. In highly industrialized states, like America, there is a tendency towards equalization of income. There is a tendency for the unskilled workman to be paid as much as the skilled—or rather, since the machine tool is abolishing the difference between them, for skilled and unskilled to fuse into a single semi-skilled type with a given standard of wages—and for the manual worker to be paid as much as the professional man. (As things stand, he is often paid more than the professional. A constructional engineer over-seeing the building of an American skyscraper may actually be paid less than a plasterer at work on the interior walls of the building. Bricklayers, earn more than many doctors, draughts-men, analytical chemists, teachers, and the like. This is partly due to the fact that the manual workers are more numerous and better organised than the brain workers and are in a better position to bargain with the capitalists; partly to the overcrowd-ing of the professions with the finished products of an educational system that turns out more would-be brain workers than there are places to fill—or for that matter than there are brains to work!) But to return to our transmogrified Proletariat. The equalization of income—that happy consummation from which Mr Bernard Shaw expects all blessings automatically to flow—is in process of being realized under the capitalist system in America. What the immediate future promises is a vast plateau of standardized income—the plateau being composed of manual labourers and the bulk of the class of clerks and small professional men—with a relatively small number of peaks rising from it to more or less giddy heights of opulence. On these peaks will be perched the hereditary owners of property, the directors of industry and finance, and the exceptionally able and successful professional men. Given this transformation of the Proletariat into a branch of the bourgeoisie, given this equalization—at an unprecedentedly high level, and over an area unprecedentedly wide—of standard income, the doctrines of socialism lose most of their charm, and the communist revolution becomes rather pointless. Those who inhabit paradise do not dream of yet remoter heavens (though it seems to me more than likely that they yearn rather wistfully sometimes for hell). The socialist paradise is a world where all share equally, and the fullness of every man's belly is guaranteed by the State. For the ordinary man the important items of this programme will be the equality of sharing and the fulness of the belly; he will not care who guarantees him these blessings, so long as guaranteed they are. If capitalism guarantees them, he will not dream of violently overthrowing capitalism for the sake of receiving precisely the same advantages from the socialist State. So that, if the present tendency continues, it would seem that the danger of a strictly communistic revolution in the highly developed industrial countries, like America, will disappear. What may happen, however, is a more gradual change in the present organization of capitalist society. A change for which capitalism itself will have been largely responsible. For by levelling up incomes at present low, in order that all may buy its productions, American capitalism is doing more for the democratization of society than any number of idealistic preachers of the Rights of Man. Indeed, it has transformed these famous rights and the claim that all men are equal from a polite fiction into the beginnings of a fact. In so doing, it seems to me, capitalism is preparing its own downfall— or rather the downfall of the extremely rich people who are now at the head of capitalist enterprise. For it is obvious that you cannot preach democracy, and not merely preach it, but actually give it practical realization throughout large tracts of society in terms of hard cash, without arousing in men the desire to be consistent and carry through the partial democratization of society to the end. We shall see, I believe, the realization of what seems at first sight a paradox—the imposition of complete equality as the result, not of monstrous injustice, poverty, discontent, and consequent bloody revolution, but of partial equalization and universal prosperity. Past revolutions failed to produce the perfect democracy in whose name they were always made, because the great masses of the downtrodden were too abjectly poor to be able really to imagine the possibility of being the equals of their oppressors. Only those who were already well on the road towards economic equality with their masters ever profited by these revolutions. Revolutions always benefited the already prosperous and well organized. In America, under modern capitalism, the whole Proletariat is prosperous and well organized; it is therefore in a position to feel its essential equality with its masters. It stands in the same relation with regard to the rich industrial overlords as did the English industrial and professional bourgeoisie with regard to the territorial magnates in 1832, or the lawyers, the merchants, the financiers, with regard to the French crown and its nobles in 1789. Incomes have been levelled up; automatically there will arise a demand that they should also be levelled down. If a plasterer is worth as much as a constructional engineer, an oil-driller as much as a geologist (and according to modern capitalist-democratic theory they deserve the same wage inasmuch as each is a man or, in economic language, a consumer)—if this equality is considered just in theory and consecrated in practice by the payment of equal wages, then, it is obvious, there can be no justifiable inequality between the incomes of plasterer and engineer on the one hand, and company director and stockholder on the other. Either violently or, more probably, by a gradual and more or less painless process of propaganda, pressure of public opinion, and finally legislation, incomes will be levelled down as they are now being levelled up; vast fortunes will be broken up; ownership of joint-stock companies will be more and more widely distributed, and the directors of these enterprises will be paid as much as the most unskilled workman or the most learned scientific expert in their employ, as much and no more. For why should one consumer receive more than another? No man has more than one belly to fill with food, one back to put clothes on, one posterior to sit in a motor car with. A century should see the more or less complete realization, in the industrial West, of Mr Shaw's dream of equal incomes for all.

And when the dream has been actualized, what then? Will the spectre of revolution be definitively laid and humanity live happily ever afterwards? Mr Shaw, at any rate, seems to imagine so. Only once, if I remember, in the whole length of his *Guide to Socialism* does he even suggest that man does not live by equal incomes alone; and then suggests it so slightly, so passingly, that the reader is still left with the impression that in equality of income lies the solution of every problem life has to offer. Fantastic doctrine, all the more absurd for being so apparently positivistic! For nothing could be more chimerical than the notion that Man is the same thing as the Economic Man and that the problems of life, Man's life, can be solved by any merely economic arrangement. To suppose that the equalization of income could solve these problems is only slightly less absurd than to suppose that they could be solved by the universal in-stallation of sanitary plumbing or the distribution of Ford cars to every member of the human species. That the equalization of income might in some ways be a good thing is obvious. (It might also, in others, be bad; it would mean, for example, the complete practical realization of the democratic ideal, and this in its turn would mean, almost inevitably, the apotheosis of the lowest human values and the rule, spiritual and material, of the worst men.) But good or bad, the equalization of income can no more touch the real sources of present discontent than could any other large-scale book-keeping operation, such as, for example, a scheme to make possible the purchase of every conceivable commodity by deferred payments.

The real trouble with the present social and industrial system is not that it makes some people very much richer than others, but that it makes life fundamentally unlivable for all. Now that not only work, but also leisure has been completely mechanized; now that, with every fresh elaboration of the social organization, the individual finds himself yet further degraded from manhood towards the mere embodiment of a social function; now that ready-made, creation-saving amusements are spreading an ever intenser boredom through ever wider spheres,—existence has becomes pointless and intolerable. Quite how pointless and how intolerable the great masses of materially-civilized humanity have not yet consciously realized. Only the more intelligent have consciously realized it as yet. To this realization the reaction of those whose intelligence is unaccompanied by some talent, some inner urge towards creation, is an intense hatred, a longing to destroy. This type of intelligent hater-of-everything has been admirably, and terrifyingly, portrayed by M. André Malraux in his novel, *Les Conquérants*. I recommend it to all sociologists.

The time is not far off when the whole population and not merely a few exceptionally intelligent individuals will consciously realize the fundamental unlivableness of life under the present régime. And what then? Consult M. Malraux. The revolution that will then break out will not be communistic—there will be no need for such a revolution, as I have already shown, and besides nobody will believe in the betterment of humanity or in anything else whatever. It will be a nihilist revolution. Destruction for destruction's sake. Hate, universal hate, and an aimless and therefore complete and thorough smashing up of everything. And the levelling up of incomes, by accelerating the spread of universal mechanization (machinery is costly), will merely accelerate the coming of this great orgy of universal nihilism. The richer, the more materially civilized we become, the more speedily it will arrive. All that we can hope is that it will not come in our time.

VULGARITY IN LITERATURE

(1930) (*an extract*)

§ 1

THE difficulty, when one is using words of appraisal, the difficulty of knowing what one means!

Then why, if it is so hard, make any attempt to know? Would it not be wiser to follow the example of that Geneva Conference convened, not long ago, to consider means for the suppression of the traffic in obscene publications? For when the Greek delegate (too Socratic by half) suggested that it might be a good thing to establish a preliminary definition of the word 'obscene', Sir Archibald Bodkin sprang to his feet with a protest. 'There is no definition of indecent or obscene in English Statute Law.' The law of other countries being, apparently, no more explicit, it was unanimously decided that no definition was possible. After which, having triumphantly asserted that they did not know what they were talking about, the members of the Congress settled down to their discussion.

My business is not with the obscene, but with the vulgar. When I call something or somebody 'vulgar', what *precisely* (as Mr T. S. Eliot would critically ask) am I saying? Rushing in where Sir Archibald and his colleagues so wisely feared to tread, I shall try to discover.

To begin with, then, I find that there are many occasions when, strictly speaking, I *mean* nothing at all, but am using the word merely to express a dislike—as a term of abuse, a politer synonym, shall we say, of 'bloody'. On such occasions 'vulgar' is no more than a vaguely pejorative noise. More often, however, I find that I intend to *say* something when I employ the word, not merely to snarl.

In certain circumstances, for example, I use the word in its strict etymological sense. When I say that a man has a vulgar accent or vulgar table manner, I mean that his accent and his manners remind me of those current in the lower ranks of society—of the particular society in which I happen to live. For vulgar here is not necessarily vulgar there. *Eructavit cor meum.* East of Constantinople, the action is said to be polite. Here, Sir Toby Belch, though a knight, can never have moved in the highest circles. Or, yes; on second thoughts, he conceivably might have. For the standards of vulgarity are seen to change as you move vertically upwards through the strata of a single society, just as they change before the eyes of a spectator moving horizontally from one society to another. What is vulgar on high level A may have ceased to be vulgar on the yet higher level B. There are refinements beyond refinements, almost *ad infinitum.* Like Paradise, the *Monde* itself has its high and low. Proust is the Dante of these high mundane spheres; but while it took several centuries to reduce Dante's guide-book to out-of-date-ness, Proust's is already, in its factual details (though not, of course, in its spirit), as hopelessly behind the times as a pre-war Baedeker. The social heavens are for ever changing.

But these relativities are too obvious to be very interesting. The Absolute chimerically beckons; and, though we can never hope to come up with it, the chase may be amusing in itself and, who knows? by the way we may actually catch a hare or two, smaller indeed and less noble than the quarry we are after, but having at least the merit of solidly existing, of being visibly there.

We have considered, so far, two cases: the case in which the word 'vulgar' says, 'I don't like this', and the case in which it says, 'This reminds me of what are, to me, the lower classes.' In the case we are about to consider now, 'vulgar' says something less easily definable. For instance, I can assert that 'this man is vulgar. The fact that he is of good family and was educated at the right places makes no difference. He is vulgar, intrinsically.' What *precisely* do I mean here?

Etymology is helpful even in this case. The vulgar man of good family is not, indeed, a member of the lower classes in our actual society. But there is an ideal society, in which, we feel, he and his like belong to some very squalid caste.

No values, except perhaps the most rudimentary biological values, are accepted by all human beings. Only the tendency to evaluate is universal. In other words, the machinery for creating values is given, but the values themselves must be manufactured. The process has not yet been rationalized; value-making is still a village industry. Among the educated classes in the West, however, values are sufficiently nearly standardized for us to be able to speak about the ideal society as though it were an absolute.

The extremes of vulgarity are as rare as the extremes of goodness, wickedness, or genius; but it happens occasionally that we meet a nature's non-gentleman who is obviously one of the pariahs of our ideal society. Such people are, intrinsically, what those wretched Indians who sweep the floor and empty the slops are by accident—untouchable. In India, when you leave your hotel and want to tip the sweeper, you must not hold out the coin, expecting him to take it. His immediate reaction to your gesture will be to shrink away; for if your fingers were to touch his receiving palm you would be defiled. He is considerately sparing you the trouble of having to take a bath, fumigate yourself, and change your underclothing. The tipping of sweepers has its own special technique; you must halt several yards away from your expectant beneficiary and throw your gift on to the ground at his feet. Commercial transactions during the Black Death must have been carried on in much the same style.

Training has taught the accidentally untouchable Indian to realize his own defiling lowness and to act accordingly. Would that nature had done the same for the intrinsic outcastes of our ideal society! But, alas, she hasn't. You find yourself at dinner sitting next to X, the eminent politician; the journalist, Y, is at large and invites you to his favourite public house. Unlike the sweepers of India, these intrinsic outcastes do not play their untouchable's part. So far are they from knowing their places, that they actually think they are doing you an honour by sitting at your table, a kindness by offering you, before lunch and in some stinking bar parlour, a double whisky or a noggin of glutinous port. As for shrinking, they do not dream of it; on the contrary, they push themselves forward. Indeed, a certain loud self-satisfaction (which renders it impossible for one to feel much sympathy with the intrinsic untouchable in his affliction), a certain thrusting and pretentious vanity is, as I shall have many occasions of showing in the course of these digressions, one of the essential elements of vulgarity. Vulgarity is a lowness that proclaims itself—and the self-proclamation is also intrinsically a lowness. For pretentiousness in whatever field, unless more than justified by native capacity and demonstrable achievement, is low in itself. Moreover, it underlines all other deficiencies and, as a suitable chemical will reveal words written in invisible ink, calls out the latent lownesses in a character, so that they manifest themselves in the form of open vulgarities.

There is a vulgarity in the sphere of morals, a vulgarity of emotions and intellect, a vulgarity even of the spirit. A man can be wicked, or stupid, or passionate without being vulgar. He can also be vulgarly good, vulgarly intelligent, vulgarly emotional or unemotional, vulgarly spiritual. Moreover, he can belong to the highest class in one sphere of activity and yet be low in another. I have known men of the greatest intellectual refinement, whose emotional life was repugnantly vulgar. Each one of us is like the population of a town built on the slope of a hill: we exist simultaneously at many different levels.

These brief notes on personal vulgarity are meant to serve as an introduction to what I propose to say about vulgarity in literature. Letters, life—the two worlds are parallel. What is true here is true, with a difference, there. For the sake of completeness I ought, of course, to have illustrated my generalizations about vulgarity in life with concrete examples. But this would have meant an excursion into the realm of fiction, or historical biography—or contemporary libel. I should have had to create a set of artistically living characters, with the circumstances of their existence. World and time, as usual, were lacking. Besides, as it happens, I have, in several works of fiction, elaborately exemplified emotional and intellectual vulgarity as revealed in life—perhaps also, without meaning to, as they are revealed in letters! I shall not begin again here. Here the ready-made examples of vulgarity provided by literature will serve, retrospectively and by analogy, to illustrate my generalizations about vulgarity in life.

§ IV

It was vulgar at the beginning of the nineteenth century to mention the word 'handkerchief' on the French tragic stage. An arbitrary convention had decreed that tragic personages must inhabit a world, in which noses exist only to distinguish the noble Romans from the Greeks and Hebrews, never to be blown. Arbitrary conventions of one sort or another are essential to art. But as the sort of convention constantly varies, so does the corresponding vulgarity. We are back among the relativities.

In the case of the handkerchief we have a particular and rather absurd application of a very widely accepted artistic convention. This convention is justified by the ancient metaphysical doctrine, which distinguishes in the universe two principles, mind and matter, and which attributes to mind an immeasurable superiority. In the name of this principle many religions have demanded the sacrifice of the body; their devotees have responded by mortifying the flesh and, in extreme cases, by committing self-castration and even suicide. Literature has its Manichaeans as well as religion: men who on principle would exile the body and its functions from the world of their art, who condemn as vulgar all too particular and detailed accounts of physical actuality, as vulgar any attempt to relate mental or spiritual events to happenings in the body. The inhabitants of their universe are not human beings, but the tragical heroes and heroines who never blow their noses.

Artistically, the abolition of handkerchiefs and all that handkerchiefs directly or indirectly stand for has certain advantages. The handkerchiefless world of pure mind and spirit is, for an adult, the nearest approach to that infinitely comfortable Freudian womb, towards which, as towards a lost paradise, we are always nostalgically yearning. In the handkerchiefless mental

world we are at liberty to work things out to their logical conclusions, we can guarantee the triumph of justice, we can control
the weather and (in the words of those yearning popular songs
which are the national anthems of Wombland) make our
Dreams come True by living under Skies of Blue with You.
Nature in the mental world is not that collection of tiresomely
opaque and recalcitrant objects, so bewildering to the man of
science, so malignantly hostile to the man of action; it is the
luminously rational substance of a Hegelian nature-philosophy,
a symbolic manifestation of the principles of dialectic. Artistically, such a Nature is much more satisfactory (because so much
more easy to deal with) than the queer, rather sinister and finally
quite incomprehensible monster, by which, when we venture
out of our ivory towers, we are instantly swallowed. And man,
than whom, as Sophocles long since remarked, nothing is more
monstrous, more marvellous, more terrifyingly strange (it is
hard to find a single word to render his *deinoteron*)—man, too,
is a very unsatisfactory subject for literature. For this creature
of inconsistencies can live on too many planes of existence. He
is the inhabitant of a kind of psychological Woolworth Building;
you never know—he never knows himself—which floor he'll
step out at tomorrow, nor even whether, a minute from now,
he won't take it into his head to jump into the elevator and shoot
up a dozen or down perhaps twenty storeys into some totally
different mode of being. The effect of the Manichaean con-
demnation of the body is at once to reduce this impossible skyscraper to less than half its original height. Confined henceforward to the mental floors of his being, man becomes an almost
easily manageable subject for the writer. In the French tragedies
(the most completely Manichaean works of art ever created) lust
itself has ceased to be corporeal and takes its place among the
other abstract symbols, with which the authors write their strange
algebraical equations of passion and conflict. The beauty of
algebraical symbols lies in their universality; they stand not for
one particular case, but for all cases. Manichaeans, the classical
writers confined themselves exclusively to the study of man as a

creature of pure reason and discarnate passions. Now the body particularizes and separates, the mind unites. By the very act of imposing limitations the classicists were enabled to achieve a certain universality of statement impossible to those who attempt to reproduce the particularities and incompleteness of actual corporeal life. But what they gained in universality, they lost in vivacity and immediate truth. You cannot get something for nothing. Some people think that universality can be paid for too highly.

To enforce their ascetic code the classicists had to devise a system of critical sanctions. Chief among these was the stigma of vulgarity attached to all those who insisted too minutely on the physical side of man's existence. Speak of handkerchiefs in a tragedy? The solecism was as monstrous as picking teeth with a fork.

At a dinner party in Paris not long ago I found myself sitting next to a French Professor of English, who assured me in the course of an otherwise very agreeable conversation that I was a leading member of the Neo-Classic school and that it was as a leading member of the Neo-Classic school that I was lectured about to the advanced students of contemporary English literature under his tutelage. The news depressed me. Classified, like a museum specimen, and lectured about, I felt most dismally posthumous. But that was not all. The thought that I was a Neo-Classic preyed upon my mind—a Neo-Classic without knowing it, a Neo-Classic against all my desires and intentions. For I have never had the smallest ambition to be a Classic of any kind, whether Neo, Palaeo, Proto or Eo. Not at any price. For, to begin with, I have a taste for the lively, the mixed, and the incomplete in art, preferring it to the universal and the chemically pure. In the second place, I regard the classical discipline, with its insistence on elimination, concentration, simplification, as being, for all the formal difficulties it imposes on the writer, essentially an escape from, a getting out of, the greatest difficulty —which is to render adequately, in terms of literature, that infinitely complex and mysterious thing, actual reality. The world of mind is a comfortable Wombland, a place to which we flee from the bewildering queerness and multiplicity of the actual world. Matter is incomparably subtler and more intricate than mind. Or, to put it a little more philosophically, the consciousness of events which we have immediately, through our senses and intuitions and feelings, is incomparably subtler than any idea we can subsequently form of that immediate consciousness. Our most refined theories, our most elaborate descriptions are but crude and barbarous simplifications of a reality that is, in every smallest sample, infinitely complex. Now, simplifications must, of course, be made; if they were not, it would be quite impossible to deal artistically (or, for that matter, scientifically) with reality at all. What is the smallest amount of simplification compatible with comprehensibility, compatible with the expression of a humanly significant meaning? It is the business of the non-classical naturalistic writer to discover. His ambition is to render, in literary terms, the quality of immediate experience —in other words, to express the finally inexpressible. To come anywhere near achieving this impossibility is much more difficult, it seems to me, than, by eliminating and simplifying, to achieve the perfectly realizable classical ideal. The cutting out of all the complex particularities of a situation (which means, as we have seen, the cutting out of all that is corporeal in it) strikes me as mere artistic shirking. But I disapprove of the shirking of artistic difficulties. Therefore I find myself disapproving of classicism.

Literature is also philosophy, is also science. In terms of beauty it enunciates truths. The beauty-truths of the best classical works possess, as we have seen, a certain algebraic universality of significance. Naturalistic works contain the more detailed beauty-truths of particular observation. These beauty-truths of art are truly scientific. All that modern psychologists, for example, have done is to systematize and de-beautify the vast treasures of knowledge about the human soul contained in novel, play, poem and essay. Writers like Blake and Shakespeare, like Stendhal and Dostoevsky, still have plenty to teach the modern scientific professional. There is a rich scientific harvest to be reaped in the works even of minor writers. By nature a natural historian, I am ambitious to add my quota to the sum of particularized beauty-truths about man and his relations with the world about him. (Incidentally, this world of relationships, this borderland between 'subjective' and 'objective' is one which literature is peculiarly, perhaps uniquely, well fitted to explore.) I do not want to be a Classical, or even a Neo-Classical, eliminator and generalizer.

This means, among other things, that I cannot accept the Classicists' excommunication of the body. I think it not only permissible, but necessary, that literature should take cognizance of physiology and should investigate the still obscure relations between the mind and its body. True, many people find the reports of such investigations, when not concealed in scientific text-books and couched in the decent obscurity of a Graeco-Latin jargon, extremely and inexcusably vulgar; and many more find them downright wicked. I myself have frequently been accused, by reviewers in public and by unprofessional readers in private correspondence, both of vulgarity and of wickedness—on the grounds, so far as I have ever been able to discover, that I reported my investigations into certain phenomena in plain English and in a novel. The fact that many people should be shocked by what he writes practically imposes it as a duty upon the writer to go on shocking them. For those who are shocked by truth are not only stupid, but morally reprehensible as well; the stupid should be educated, the wicked punished and reformed. All these praiseworthy ends can be attained by a course of shocking; retributive pain will be inflicted on the truth-haters by the first shocking truths, whose repetition will gradually build up in those who read them an immunity to pain and will end by reforming and educating the stupid criminals out of their truth-hating. For a familiar truth ceases to shock. To render it familiar is therefore a duty. It is also a pleasure. For, as Baudelaire says, *'ce qu'il y a d'enivrant dans le mauvais goût, c'est le plaisir aristocratique de déplaire.'*

§ VI

Eulalie, Ulalume, Raven and Bells, Conqueror Worm and Haunted Palace. . . . Was Edgar Allan Poe a major poet? It would surely never occur to any English-speaking critic to say so. And yet, in France, from 1850 till the present time, the best poets of each generation—yes, and the best critics, too; for, like most excellent poets, Baudelaire, Mallarmé, Paul Valéry are also admirable critics—have gone out of their way to praise him. Only a year or two ago M. Valéry repeated the now traditional French encomium of Poe, and added at the same time a protest against the faintness of our English praise. We who are speakers of English and not English scholars, who were born into the language and from childhood have been pickled in its literature —we can only say, with all due respect, that Baudelaire, Mallarmé and Valéry are wrong and that Poe is not one of our major poets. A taint of vulgarity spoils, for the English reader, all but two or three of his poems—the marvellous 'City in the Sea' and 'To Helen', for example, whose beauty and crystal perfection make us realize, as we read them, what a very great artist perished on most of the occasions when Poe wrote verse. It is to this perished artist that the French poets pay their tribute. Not being English they are incapable of appreciating those finer shades of vulgarity that ruin Poe for us, just as we, not being French, are incapable of appreciating those finer shades of lyrical beauty which are, for them, the making of La Fontaine.

The substance of Poe is refined; it is his form that is vulgar. He is, as it were, one of Nature's Gentlemen, unhappily cursed with incorrigible bad taste. To the most sensitive and high-souled man in the world we should find it hard to forgive, shall we say, the wearing of a diamond ring on every finger. Poe does the equivalent of this in his poetry; we notice the solecism and shudder. Foreign observers do not notice it; they detect only the native gentlemanliness in the poetical intention, not the vulgarity in the details of execution. To them, we seem perversely and quite incomprehensibly unjust.

It is when Poe tries to make it too poetical that his poetry takes on its peculiar tinge of badness. Protesting too much that he is a gentleman, and opulent into the bargain, he falls into vulgarity. Diamond rings on every finger proclaim the parvenu.

Consider, for example, the first two stanzas of 'Ulalume'.

> The skies they were ashen and sober;
>> The leaves they were crisped and sere—
>> The leaves they were withering and sere;
> It was night in the lonesome October
>> Of my most immemorial year;
> It was hard by the dim lake of Auber,
>> In the misty mid region of Weir—
> It was down by the dank tarn of Auber
>> In the ghoul-haunted woodland of Weir.
>
> Here once, through an alley Titanic,
>> Of cypress, I roamed with my soul,
>> Of cypress, with Psyche my soul.
> These were the days when my heart was volcanic
>> As the scoriac rivers that roll—
>> As the lavas that restlessly roll
> Their sulphurous currents down Yaanek
>> In the ultimate clime of the pole—
> That groan as they roll down Mount Yaanek
>> In the realms of the boreal pole.

These lines protest too much (and with what a variety of voices!) that they are poetical, and, protesting, are therefore vulgar. To start with, the walloping dactylic metre is all too musical. Poetry ought to be musical, but musical with tact, subtly and variously. Metres whose rhythms, as in this case, are strong, insistent and practically invariable offer the poet a kind of short cut to musicality. They provide him (my subject calls for a mixture of metaphors) with a ready-made, reach-me-down music. He does

not have to create a music appropriately modulated to his meaning; all he has to do is to shovel the meaning into the moving
stream of the metre and allow the current to carry it along on
waves that, like those of the best hairdressers, are guaranteed
permanent. Many nineteenth-century poets used these metrical
short cuts to music, with artistically fatal results.

> Then when nature around me is smiling
>> The last smile which answers to mine,
> I do not believe in beguiling,
>> Because it reminds me of thine.

How can one take Byron seriously, when he protests his
musicalness in such loud and vulgar accents? It is only by luck
or an almost superhuman poetical skill that these all too musical
metres can be made to sound, through their insistent barrel-
organ rhythms, the intricate, personal music of the poet's own
meaning. Byron occasionally, for a line or two, takes the hard
kink out of those dactylic permanent waves and appears, so to
speak, in his own musical hair; and Hood, by an unparalleled
prodigy of technique, turns even the reach-me-down music of
'The Bridge of Sighs' into a personal music, made to the measure
of the subject and his own emotion. Moore, on the contrary, is
always perfectly content with the permanent wave; and Swin-
burne, that super-Moore of a later generation, was also content
to be a permanent waver—the most accomplished, perhaps, in
all the history of literature. The complexity of his ready-made
musics and his technical skill in varying the number, shape and
contour of his permanent waves are simply astonishing. But, like
Poe and the others, he protested too much, he tried to be too
poetical. However elaborately devious his short cuts to music
may be, they are still short cuts—and short cuts (this is the
irony) to poetical vulgarity.

A quotation and a parody will illustrate the difference between
ready-made music and music made to measure. I remember (I
trust correctly) a simile of Milton's:—

> Like that fair field
> Of Enna, where Proserpine gathering flowers,
> Herself a fairer flower, by gloomy Dis
> Was gathered, which cost Ceres all that pain
> To seek her through the world.

Rearranged according to their musical phrasing, these lines would have to be written thus:—

> Like that fair field of Enna,
> where Proserpine gathering flowers,
> Herself a fairer flower,
> by gloomy Dis was gathered,
> Which cost Ceres all that pain
> To seek her through the world.

The contrast between the lyrical swiftness of the first four phrases, with that row of limping spondees which tells of Ceres' pain, is thrillingly appropriate. Bespoke, the music fits the sense like a glove.

How would Poe have written on the same theme? I have ventured to invent his opening stanza.

> It was noon in the fair field of Enna,
> When Proserpina gathering flowers—
> Herself the most fragrant of flowers,
> Was gathered away to Gehenna
>
> By the Prince of Plutonian powers;
> Was borne down the windings of Brenner
> To the gloom of his amorous bowers—
> Down the tortuous highway of Brenner
> To the god's agapemonous bowers.

The parody is not too outrageous to be critically beside the point; and anyhow the music is genuine Poe. That permanent wave is unquestionably an *ondulation de chez Edgar*. The much too musical metre is (to change the metaphor once more) like a rich chasuble, so stiff with gold and gems that it stands un-supported, a carapace of jewelled sound, into which the sense, like some snotty little seminarist, irrelevantly creeps and is lost. This music of Poe's—how much less really musical it is than that which, out of his nearly neutral decasyllables, Milton fashioned on purpose to fit the slender beauty of Proserpine, the strength and swiftness of the ravisher and her mother's heavy, despairing sorrow!

Of the versification of 'The Raven' Poe says, in his *Philosophy of Composition*: 'My first object (as usual) was originality. The extent to which this has been neglected in versification is one of the most unaccountable things in the world. Admitting that there is little possibility of variety in mere *rhythm*, it is still clear that the possible varieties of metre and stanza are absolutely infinite—and yet, *for centuries, no man, in verse, has ever done or ever seemed to think of doing an original thing.*' This fact, which Poe hardly exaggerates, speaks volumes for the good sense of the poets. Feeling that almost all strikingly original metres and stanzas were only illegitimate short cuts to a music which, when reached, turned out to be but a poor and vulgar substitute for individual music, they wisely stuck to the less blatantly musical metres of tradition. The ordinary iambic decasyllable, for ex-ample, is intrinsically musical enough to be just able, when required, to stand up by itself. But its musical stiffness can easily be taken out of it. It can be now a chasuble, a golden carapace of sound, now, if the poet so desires, a pliant, soft and, musically speaking, almost neutral material, out of which he can fashion a special music of his own to fit his thoughts and feelings in all their incessant transformations. Good landscape painters seldom choose a 'picturesque' subject; they want to paint their own picture, not have it imposed on them by nature. In the thor-oughly paintable little places of this world you will generally find only bad painters. (It's so easy to paint the thoroughly paintable.) The good ones prefer the unspectacular neutralities of the Home Counties to those Cornish coves and Ligurian fishing villages, whose picturesqueness is the delight of all those who have no pictures of their own to project on to the canvas. It is the same with poetry: good poets avoid what I may call, by analogy, 'musicesque' metres, preferring to create their own music out of raw materials as nearly as possible neutral. Only bad poets, or good poets against their better judgment, and by mistake, go to the Musicesque for their material. 'For centuries no man, in verse, had ever done or ever seemed to think of doing an original thing.' It remained for Poe and the other nineteenth-century metrists to do it; Procrustes-like, they tortured and amputated significance into fitting the ready-made music of their highly original metres and stanzas. The result was, in most cases, as vulgar as a Royal Academy Sunrise on Ben Nevis (with Highland Cattle) or a genuine hand-painted sketch of Portofino.

§ VII

It is vulgar, in literature, to make a display of emotions which you do not naturally have, but think you ought to have, because all the best people do have them. It is also vulgar (and this is the more common case) to have emotions, but to express them so badly, with so many too many protestings, that you seem to have no natural feelings, but to be merely fabricating emotions by a process of literary forgery. Sincerity in art, as I have pointed out elsewhere, is mainly a matter of talent. Keats's love letters ring true, because he had great literary gifts. Most men and women are capable of feeling passion, but not of expressing it; their love letters (as we learn from the specimens read aloud at inquests and murder trials, in the divorce court, during breach of promise cases) are either tritely flat or tritely bombastic. In either case manifestly insincere, and in the second case also vulgar—for to protest too much is always vulgar, when the protestations are so incompetent as not to carry conviction. And perhaps such excessive protestations can never be convincing, however accomplished the protester.

The case of Dickens is a strange one. The really monstrous emotional vulgarity, of which he is guilty now and then in all his books and almost continuously in *The Old Curiosity Shop*, is

H

not the emotional vulgarity of one who simulates feelings which he does not have. It is evident, on the contrary, that Dickens felt most poignantly for and with his Little Nell; that he wept over her sufferings, piously revered her goodness and exulted in her joys. He had an overflowing heart; but the trouble was that it overflowed with such curious and even rather repellant secretions. The creator of the later Pickwick and the Cheeryble Brothers, of Tim Linkinwater the bachelor and Mr Garland and so many other gruesome old Peter Pans was obviously a little abnormal in his emotional reactions. There was something rather wrong with a man who could take this lachrymose and tremulous pleasure in adult infantility. He would doubtless have justified his rather frightful emotional taste by a reference to the New Testament. But the child-like qualities of character commended by Jesus are certainly not the same as those which distinguish the old infants in Dicken's novels. There is all the difference in the world between infants and children. Infants are stupid and unaware and sub-human. Children are remarkable for their intelligence and ardour, for their curiosity, their intolerance of shams, the clarity and ruthlessness of their vision. From all accounts Jesus must have been child-like, not at all infantile. A child-like man is not a man whose development has been arrested; on the contrary, he is a man who had given himself a chance of continuing to develop long after most adults have muffled themselves in the cocoon of middle-aged habit and convention. An infantile man is one who has not developed at all, or who has regressed towards the womb, into a comfortable unawareness. So far from being attractive and commendable, an infantile man is really a most repulsive, because a truly monstrous and misshapen, being. A writer who can tearfully adore these stout or cadaverous old babies, snugly ensconced in their mental and economic womb-substitutes and sucking, between false teeth, their thumbs, must have something seriously amiss with his emotional constitution.

One of Dickens's most striking peculiarities is that, whenever in his writing he becomes emotional, he ceases instantly to use his intelligence. The overflowing of his heart drowns his head and even dims his eyes; for, whenever he is in the melting mood, Dickens ceases to be able and probably ceases even to wish to see reality. His one and only desire on these occasions is just to overflow, nothing else. Which he does, with a vengeance and in an atrocious blank verse that is meant to be poetical prose and succeeds only in being the worst kind of fustian. 'When Death strikes down the innocent and young, from every fragile form from which he lets the panting spirit free, a hundred virtues rise, in shapes of mercy, charity and love, to walk the world and bless it. Of every tear that sorrowing mortals shed on such green graves, some good is born, some gentler nature comes. In the Destroyer's steps there spring up bright creations that defy his power, and his dark path becomes a way of light to Heaven.' And so on, a stanchless flux.

Mentally drowned and blinded by the sticky overflowings of his heart, Dickens was incapable, when moved, of re-creating, in terms of art, the reality which had moved him, was even, it would seem, unable to perceive that reality. Little Nelly's sufferings and death distressed him as, in real life, they would distress any normally constituted man; for the suffering and death of children raise the problem of evil in its most unanswerable form. It was Dickens's business as a writer to re-create in terms of his art this distressing reality. He failed. The history of Little Nell is distressing indeed, but not as Dickens presumably meant it to be distressing; it is distressing in its ineptitude and vulgar sentimentality.

A child, Ilusha, suffers and dies in Dostoevsky's *Brothers Karamazov*. Why is this history so agonizingly moving, when the tale of Little Nell leaves us not merely cold, but derisive? Comparing the two stories, we are instantly struck by the incomparably greater richness in factual detail of Dostoevsky's creation. Feeling did not prevent him from seeing and recording, or rather recreating. All that happened round Ilusha's deathbed he saw, unerringly. The emotion-blinded Dickens noticed practically nothing of what went on in Little Nelly's neighbourhood during the child's last days. We are almost forced, indeed, to believe that he didn't want to see anything. He wanted to be unaware himself and he wanted his readers to be unaware of everything except Little Nell's sufferings on the one hand and her goodness and innocence on the other. But goodness and innocence and the undeservedness of suffering and even, to some extent, suffering itself are only significant in relation to the actual realities of human life. Isolated, they cease to mean anything, perhaps to exist. Even the classical writers surrounded their abstract and algebraical personages with at least the abstract and algebraical implication of the human realities, in relation to which virtues and vices are significant. Thanks to Dickens's pathologically deliberate unawareness, Nell's virtues are marooned, as it were, in the midst of a boundless waste of unreality; isolated, they fade and die. Even her sufferings and death lack significance because of this isolation. Dickens's unawareness was the death of death itself. Unawareness, according to the ethics of Buddhism, is one of the deadly sins. The stupid are wicked. (Incidentally, the cleverest men can, sometimes and in certain circumstances, reveal themselves as profoundly—criminally—stupid. You can be an acute logician and at the same time an emotional cretin.) Damned in the realm of conduct, the unaware are also damned aesthetically. Their art is bad; instead of creating, they murder.

Art, as I have said, is also philosophy, is also science. Other things being equal, the work of art, which in its own way 'says' more about the universe will be better than the work of art which says less. (The 'other things' which have to be equal are the forms of beauty, in terms of which the artist must express his philosophic and scientific truths.) Why is *The Rosary* a less admirable novel than *The Brothers Karamazov?* Because the amount of experience of all kinds understood, 'felt into,' as the Germans would say, and artistically re-created by Mrs Barclay is small in comparison with that which Doestovsky feelingly comprehended and knew so consummately well how to re-create in terms of the novelist's art. Dostoevsky covers all Mrs Barclay's ground and a vast area beside. The pathetic parts of *The Old Curiosity Shop* are as poor in understood and artistically re-created experience as *The Rosary*—indeed, I think they are even poorer. At the same time they are vulgar (which *The Rosary*, that genuine masterpiece of the servant's hall, is not). They are vulgar, because their poverty is a pretentious poverty, because their disease (for the quality of Dickens's sentimentality is truly pathological) professes to be the most radiant health; because they protest their unintelligence, their lack of under-standing with a vehemence of florid utterance that is not only shocking, but ludicrous.

TRAGEDY AND THE WHOLE TRUTH

From *Music at Night* (1931)

THERE were six of them, the best and bravest of the hero's companions. Turning back from his post in the bows, Odysseus was in time to see them lifted, struggling, into the air, to hear their screams, the desperate repetition of his own name. The survivors could only look on, helplessly, while Scylla 'at the mouth of the cave devoured them, still screaming, still stretching out their hands to me in the frightful struggle.' And Odysseus adds that it was the most dreadful and lamentable sight he ever saw in all his 'explorings of the passes of the sea'. We can believe it; Homer's brief description (the too poetical simile is a later interpolation) convinces us.

Later, the danger passed, Odysseus and his men went ashore for the night, and, on the Sicilian beach, prepared their supper—prepared it, says Homer, 'expertly'. The Twelfth Book of the *Odyssey* concludes with these words: 'When they had satisfied their thirst and hunger, they thought of their dear companions and wept, and in the midst of their tears sleep came gently upon them.'

The truth, the whole truth and nothing but the truth—how rarely the older literatures ever told it! Bits of the truth, yes; every good book gives us bits of the truth, would not be a good book if it did not. But the whole truth, no. Of the great writers of the past incredibly few have given us that. Homer—the Homer of the *Odyssey*—is one of those few.

'Truth?' you question. 'For example, $2+2=4$? Or Queen Victoria came to the throne in 1837? Or light travels at the rate of 187,000 miles a second?' No, obviously, you won't find much of that sort of thing in literature. The 'truth' of which I was speaking just now is in fact no more than an acceptable verisimilitude. When the experiences recorded in a piece of literature correspond fairly closely with our own actual experiences or with what I may call our potential experiences—experiences, that is to say, which we feel (as the result of a more or less explicit process of inference from known facts) that we might have had —we say, inaccurately no doubt: 'This piece of writing is true.' But this, of course, is not the whole story. The record of a case in a text-book of psychology is scientifically true, in so far as it is an accurate account of particular events. But it might also strike the reader as being 'true' with regard to himself—that is to say, acceptable, probable, having a correspondence with his own actual or potential experiences. But a text-book of psychology is not a work of art—or only secondarily and incidentally a work of art. Mere verisimilitude, mere correspondence of experience recorded by the writer with experience remembered or imaginable by the reader, is not enough to make a work of art seem 'true'. Good art possesses a kind of super-truth—is more probable, more acceptable, more convincing than fact itself. Naturally; for the artist is endowed with a sensibility and a power of communication, a capacity to 'put things across', which events and the majority of people to whom events happen, do not possess. Experience teaches only the teachable, who are by no means as numerous as Mrs Micawber's papa's favourite proverb would lead us to suppose. Artists are eminently teachable and also eminently teachers. They receive from events much more than most men receive, and they can transmit what they have received with a peculiar penetrative force, which drives their communication deep into the reader's mind. One of our most ordinary reactions to a good piece of literary art is expressed in the formula: 'This is what I have always felt and thought, but have never been able to put clearly into words, even for myself.'

We are now in a position to explain what we mean when we say that Homer is a writer who tells the Whole Truth. We mean that the experiences he records correspond fairly closely with our own actual or potential experiences—and correspond with our experiences not on a single limited sector, but all along the line of our physical and spiritual being. And we also mean that

Homer records these experiences with a penetrative artistic force that makes them seem peculiarly acceptable and convincing.

So much, then, for truth in literature. Homer's, I repeat, is the Whole Truth. Consider how almost any other of the great poets would have concluded the story of Scylla's attack on the passing ship. Six men, remember, have been taken and devoured before the eyes of their friends. In any other poem but the *Odyssey*, what would the survivors have done? They would, of course, have wept, even as Homer made them weep. But would they previously have cooked their supper, and cooked it, what's more, in a masterly fashion? Would they previously have drunk and eaten to satiety? And after weeping, or actually while weeping, would they have dropped quietly off to sleep? No, they most certainly would not have done any of these things. They would simply have wept, lamenting their own misfortune and the horrible fate of their companions, and the canto would have ended tragically on their tears.

Homer, however, preferred to tell the Whole Truth. He knew that even the most cruelly bereaved must eat; that hunger is stronger than sorrow and that its satisfaction takes precedence even of tears. He knew that experts continue to act expertly and to find satisfaction in their accomplishment, even when friends have just been eaten, even when the accomplishment is only cooking the supper. He knew that, when the belly is full (and only when the belly is full) men can afford to grieve, and that sorrow after supper is almost a luxury. And finally he knew that, even as hunger takes precedence of grief, so fatigue, supervening, cuts short its career and drowns it in a sleep all the sweeter for bringing forgetfulness of bereavement. In a word, Homer refused to treat the theme tragically. He preferred to tell the Whole Truth.

Another author who preferred to tell the Whole Truth was Fielding. *Tom Jones* is one of the very few Odyssean books written in Europe between the time of Aeschylus and the present age; Odyssean, because never tragical; never—even when painful and disastrous, even when pathetic and beautiful things are happening. For they do happen; Fielding, like Homer, admits all the facts, shirks nothing. Indeed, it is precisely because these authors shirk nothing that their books are not tragical. For among the things they don't shirk are the irrelevancies which, in actual life, always temper the situations and characters that writers of tragedy insist on keeping chemically pure. Consider, for example, the case of Sophy Western, that most charming, most nearly perfect of young women. Fielding, it is obvious, adored her (she is said to have been created in the image of his first, much-loved wife). But in spite of his adoration, he refused to turn her into one of those chemically pure and, as it were, focussed beings who do and suffer in the world of tragedy. That innkeeper who lifted the weary Sophia from her horse—what need had he to fall? In no tragedy would he (nay, *could* he) have collapsed beneath her weight. For, to begin with, in the tragical context weight is an irrelevance; heroines should be above the law of gravitation. But that is not all; let the reader now remember what were the results of his fall. Tumbling flat on his back, he pulled Sophia down on top of him—his belly was a cushion, so that happily she came to no bodily harm—pulled her down head first. But head first is necessarily legs last; there was a momentary display of the most ravishing charms; the bumpkins at the inn door grinned or guffawed; poor Sophia, when they picked her up, was blushing in an agony of embarrassment and wounded modesty. There is nothing intrinsically improbable about this incident, which is stamped, indeed, with all the marks of literary truth. But however true, it is an incident which could never, never have happened to a heroine of tragedy. It would never have been allowed to happen. But Fielding refused to impose the tragedian's veto; he shirked nothing—neither the intrusion of irrelevant absurdities into the midst of romance or disaster, nor any of life's no less irrelevantly painful interruptions of the course of happiness. He did not want to be a tragedian. And, sure enough, that brief and pearly gleam of Sophia's charming posterior was sufficient to scare the Muse of Tragedy out of *Tom Jones* just as, more than five and twenty centuries before, the sight of stricken men first eating, then remembering to weep, then forgetting their tears in slumber had scared her out of the *Odyssey*.

In his *Principles of Literary Criticism* Mr I. A. Richards affirms that good tragedy is proof against irony and irrelevance —that it can absorb anything into itself and still remain tragedy. Indeed, he seems to make of this capacity to absorb the untragical and the anti-tragical a touchstone of tragic merit. Thus tried, practically all Greek, all French and most Elizabethan tragedies are found wanting. Only the best of Shakespeare can stand the test. So, at least, says Mr Richards. Is he right? I have often had my doubts. The tragedies of Shakespeare are veined, it is true, with irony and an often terrifying cynicism; but the cynicism is always heroic idealism turned neatly inside out, the irony is a kind of photographic negative of heroic romance. Turn Troilus's white into black and all his blacks into white and you have Thersites. Reversed, Othello and Desdemona become Iago. White Ophelia's negative is the irony of Hamlet, is the ingenuous bawdry of her own mad songs; just as the cynicism of mad King Lear is the black shadow-replica of Cordelia. Now, the shadow, the photographic negative of a thing, is in no sense irrelevant to it. Shakespeare's ironies and cynicisms serve to deepen his tragic world, but not to widen it. If they had widened it, as the Homeric irrelevancies widened out the universe of the *Odyssey* —why, then, the world of Shakespearean tragedy would automatically have ceased to exist. For example, a scene showing the bereaved Macduff eating his supper, growing melancholy, over the whisky, with thoughts of his murdered wife and children, and then, with lashes still wet, dropping off to sleep, would be true enough to life; but it would not be true to tragic art. The introduction of such a scene would change the whole quality of the play; treated in this Odyssean style, *Macbeth* would cease to be a tragedy. Or take the case of Desdemona. Iago's bestially cynical remarks about her character are in no sense, as we have seen, irrelevant to the tragedy. They present us with negative images of her real nature and of the feelings she has for Othello.

These negative images are always *hers*, are always recognizably the property of the heroine-victim of a tragedy. Whereas, if, springing ashore at Cyprus, she had tumbled, as the no less exquisite Sophia was to tumble, and revealed the inadequacies of sixteenth-century underclothing, the play would no longer be the *Othello* we know. Iago might breed a family of little cynics and the existing dose of bitterness and savage negation be doubled and trebled; *Othello* would still remain fundamentally *Othello*; But a few Fieldingesque irrelevancies would destroy it —destroy it, that is to say, as a tragedy; for there would be nothing to prevent it from becoming a magnificent drama of some other kind. For the fact is that tragedy and what I have called the Whole Truth are not compatible; where one is, the other is not. There are certain things which even the best, even Shakespearean tragedy, cannot absorb into itself.

To make a tragedy the artist must isolate a single element out of the totality of human experience and use that exclusively as his material. Tragedy is something that is separated out from the Whole Truth, distilled from it, so to speak, as an essence is distilled from the living flower. Tragedy is chemically pure. Hence its power to act quickly and intensely on our feelings. All chemically pure art has this power to act upon us quickly and intensely. Thus, chemically pure pornography (on the rare occasions when it happens to be written convincingly, by some one who has the gift of 'putting things across') is a quick-acting emotional drug of incomparably greater power than the Whole Truth about sensuality, or even (for many people) than the tangible and carnal reality itself. It is because of its chemical purity that tragedy so effectively performs its function of catharsis. It refines and corrects and gives a style to our emotional life, and does so swiftly, with power. Brought into contact with tragedy, the elements of our being fall, for the moment at any rate, into an ordered and beautiful pattern, as the iron filings arrange themselves under the influence of the magnet. Through all its individual variations, this pattern is always fundamentally of the same kind. From the reading or the hearing of a tragedy we rise with the feeling that

> Our friends are exultations, agonies,
> And love, and man's unconquerable mind;

with the heroic conviction that we too would be unconquerable if subjected to the agonies, that in the midst of the agonies we too should continue to love, might even learn to exult. It is because it does these things to us that tragedy is felt to be so valuable. What are the values of Wholly-Truthful art? What does it do to us that seems worth doing? Let us try to discover.

Wholly-Truthful art overflows the limits of tragedy and shows us, if only by hints and implications, what happened before the tragic story began, what will happen after it is over, what is happening simultaneously elsewhere (and 'elsewhere' includes all those parts of the minds and bodies of the protagonists not immediately engaged in the tragic struggle.) Tragedy is an arbitrarily isolated eddy on the surface of a vast river that flows on majestically, irresistibly, around, beneath, and to either side of it. Wholly-Truthful art contrives to imply the existence of the entire river as well as of the eddy. It is quite different from tragedy, even though it may contain, among other constituents, all the elements from which tragedy is made. (The 'same thing' placed in different contexts, loses its identity and becomes, for the perceiving mind, a succession of different things.) In Wholly-Truthful art the agonies may be just as real, love and the unconquerable mind just as admirable, just as important, as in tragedy. Thus, Scylla's victims suffer as painfully as the monster-devoured Hippolytus in *Phèdre*; the mental anguish of Tom Jones when he thinks he has lost his Sophia, and lost her by his own fault, is hardly less than that of Othello after Desdemona's murder. (The fact that Fielding's power of 'putting things across' is by no means equal to Shakespeare's is, of course, merely an accident.) But the agonies and indomitabilities are placed by the Wholly-Truthful writer in another wider context, with the result that they cease to be the same as the intrinsically identical agonies and indomitabilities of tragedy. Consequently, Wholly-Truthful art produces in us an effect quite different from that produced by tragedy. Our mood when we have read a Wholly-Truthful book is never one of heroic exultation; it is one of resignation, of acceptance. (Acceptance can also be heroic.) Being chemically impure, Wholly-Truthful literature cannot move us as quickly and intensely as tragedy or any other kind of chemically pure art. But I believe that its effects are more lasting. The exultations that follow the reading or hearing of a tragedy are in the nature of temporary inebriations. Our being cannot long hold the pattern imposed by tragedy. Remove the magnet and the filings tend to fall back into confusion. But the pattern of acceptance and resignation imposed upon us by Wholly-Truthful literature, though perhaps less unexpectedly beautiful in design, is (for that very reason perhaps) more stable. The catharsis of tragedy is violent and apocalyptic; but the milder catharsis of Wholly-Truthful literature is lasting.

In recent times literature has become more and more acutely conscious of the Whole Truth—of the great oceans of irrelevant things, events and thoughts stretching endlessly away in every direction from whatever island point (a character, a story) the author may choose to contemplate. To impose the kind of arbitrary limitations, which must be imposed by any one who wants to write a tragedy, has become more and more difficult— is now indeed, for those who are at all sensitive to contemporaneity, almost impossible. This does not mean, of course, that the modern writer must confine himself to a merely naturalistic manner. One can imply the existence of the Whole Truth without laboriously cataloguing every object within sight. A book can be written in terms of pure phantasy and yet, by implication, tell the Whole Truth. Of all the important works of contemporary literature not one is a pure tragedy. There is no contemporary writer of significance who does not prefer to state or imply the Whole Truth. However different one from another in style, in ethical, philosophical and artistic intention, in the scales of values accepted, contemporary writers have this in common, that they are interested in the Whole Truth. Proust, D. H. Lawrence, André Gide, Kafka, Hemingway—here are five obviously significant and important contemporary writers. Five authors as remarkably unlike one another as they could well be. They are at one only in this: that none of them has written a pure tragedy, that all are concerned with the Whole Truth.

I have sometimes wondered whether tragedy, as a form of art, may not be doomed. But the fact that we are still profoundly moved by the tragic masterpieces of the past—that we can be moved, against our better judgment, even by the bad tragedies of the contemporary stage and film—makes me think that the day of chemically pure art is not over. Tragedy happens to be passing through a period of eclipse, because all the significant writers of our age are too busy exploring the newly discovered, or re-discovered, world of the Whole Truth to be able to pay any attention to it. But there is no good reason to believe that this state of things will last for ever. Tragedy is too valuable to be allowed to die. There is no reason, after all, why the two kinds of literature—the Chemically Impure and the Chemically Pure, the literature of the Whole Truth and the literature of Partial Truth—should not exist simultaneously, each in its separate sphere. The human spirit has need of both.

WANTED, A NEW PLEASURE

From *Music at Night* (1931)

NINETEENTH-CENTURY science discovered the technique of discovery, and our age is, in consequence, the age
of inventions. Yes, the age of inventions; we are never tired of
proclaiming the fact. The age of inventions—and yet nobody
has succeeded in inventing a new pleasure.

It was in the course of a recent visit to that region which the
Travel Agency advertisements describe as the particular home
of pleasure—the French Riviera—that this curious and rather
distressing fact first dawned on me. From the Italian frontier to
the mountains of the Esterel, forty miles of Mediterranean coast
have been turned into one vast 'pleasure resort'. Or to be more
accurate, they have been turned into one vast straggling suburb
—the suburb of all Europe and the two Americas—punctuated
here and there with urban nuclei, such as Mentone, Nice,
Antibes, Cannes. The French have a genius for elegance; but
they are also endowed with a genius for ugliness. There are no
suburbs in the world so hideous as those which surround French
cities. The great Mediterranean *banlieue* of the Riviera is no
exception to the rule. The chaotic squalor of this long bourgeois
slum is happily unique. The towns are greatly superior, of
course, to their connecting suburbs. A certain pleasingly and
absurdly old-fashioned, gimcrack grandiosity adorns Monte
Carlo; Nice is large, bright, and lively; Cannes, gravely pompous
and as though conscious of its expensive smartness. And all of
them are equipped with the most elaborate and costly apparatus
for providing their guests with pleasure.

It was while disporting myself, or rather while trying to dis-
port myself, in the midst of this apparatus, that I came to my
depressing conclusion about the absence of new pleasures. The
thought, I remember, occurred to me one dismal winter evening
as I emerged from the Restaurant des Ambassadeurs at Cannes

into one of those howling winds, half Alpine, half marine, which on certain days transform the Croisette and the Promenade des Anglais into the most painfully realistic imitations of Wuthering Heights. I suddenly realized that, so far as pleasures were concerned, we are no better off than the Romans or the Egyptians. Galileo and Newton, Faraday and Clerk Maxwell have lived, so far as human pleasures are concerned, in vain. The great joint-stock companies which control the modern pleasure industries can offer us nothing in any essential way different from the diversions which consuls offered to the Roman plebs or Trimalchio's panders could prepare for the amusement of the bored and jaded rich in the age of Nero. And this is true in spite of the movies, the talkies, the gramophone, the radio, and all similar modern apparatus for the entertainment of humanity. These instruments, it is true, are all essentially modern; nothing like them has existed before. But because the machines are modern it does not follow that the entertainments which they reproduce and broadcast are also modern. They are not. All that these new machines do is to make accessible to a larger public the drama, pantomime, and music which have from time immemorial amused the leisures of humanity.

These mechanically reproduced entertainments are cheap and are therefore not encouraged in pleasure resorts, such as those on the Riviera, which exist for the sole purpose of making travellers part with the maximum amount of money in the minimum space of time. In these places drama, pantomime, and music are therefore provided in the original form, as they were provided to our ancestors, without the interposition of any mechanical go-between. The other pleasures of the resorts are no less traditional. Eating and drinking too much; looking at half or wholly naked ballerinas and acrobats in the hope of stimulating a jaded sexual appetite; dancing; playing games and watching games, preferably rather bloody and ferocious games; killing animals—these have always been the sports of the rich and, when they had the chance, of the poor also. No less traditional is that other strange amusement so characteristic of the Riviera—gambling.

Gambling must be at least as old as money; much older, I should imagine—as old as human nature itself, or at any rate as old as boredom, as old as the craving for artificial excitement and factitious emotions.

Officially, this closes the list of pleasures provided by the Riviera entertainment industries. But it must not be forgotten that, for those who pay for them, all these pleasures are situated, so to speak, in a certain emotional field—in the pleasure-pain complex of snobbery. The fact of being able to buy admission to 'exclusive' (that is generally to say, expensive) places of entertainment gives most people a considerable satisfaction. They like to think of the poor and vulgar herd outside, just as, according to Tertullian and many other Fathers of the Church, the Blessed enjoy looking down from the balconies of Heaven on to the writhings of the Damned in the pit below. They like to feel, with a certain swelling of pride, that they are sitting among the elect, or that they are themselves the elect, whose names figure in the social columns of the Continental *Daily Mail*, or the Paris edition of the *New York Herald*. True, snobbery is often the source of excruciating pain. But it is no less the source of exquisite pleasures. These pleasures, I repeat, are liberally provided in all the resorts and constitute a kind of background to all the other pleasures.

Now all these pleasure-resort pleasures, including those of snobbery, are immemorially antique—variations, at the best, on traditional themes. We live in the age of inventions; but the professional discoverers have been unable to think of any wholly new way of pleasurably stimulating our senses or evoking agreeable emotional reactions.

But this, I went on to reflect, as I shouldered my way through the opposing gale on the Croisette, this is not, after all, so surprising. Our physiological make-up has remained very much what it was ten thousand years ago. True, there have been considerable changes in our mode of consciousness; at no time, it is obvious, are *all* the potentialities of the human psyche simultaneously realized; history is, among many other things, the record of the successive actualization, neglect, and reactualization in another context of different sets of these almost indefinitely numerous potentialities. But in spite of these changes (which it is customary to call, incorrectly, psychic evolution), the simple instinctive feelings to which, as well as to the senses, the purveyors of pleasure make their appeal, have remained remarkably stable. The task of the pleasure merchants is to provide a sort of Highest Common Denominator of entertainment that shall satisfy large numbers of men and women, irrespective of their psychological idiosyncrasies. Such an entertainment, it is obvious, must be very unspecialized. Its appeal must be to the simplest of shared human characteristics—to the physiological and psychological foundations of personality, not to personality itself. Now, the number of appeals that can be made to what I may call the Great Impersonalities common to all human beings is strictly limited—so strictly limited that, as it has turned out, our inventors have been unable hitherto to devise any new ones. (One doubtful example of a new pleasure exists; I shall speak of it later.) We are still content with the pleasures which charmed our ancestors in the Bronze Age. (Incidentally, there are good reasons for regarding our entertainments as intrinsically inferior to those of the Bronze Age. Modern pleasures are wholly secular and without the smallest cosmic significance; whereas the entertainments of the Bronze Age were mostly religious rites and were felt by those who participated in them to be pregnant with important meanings.)

So far as I can see, the only possible new pleasure would be one derived from the invention of a new drug—of a more efficient and less harmful substitute for alcohol and cocaine. If I were a millionaire, I should endow a band of research workers to look for the ideal intoxicant. If we could sniff or swallow something that would, for five or six hours each day, abolish our solitude as individuals, atune us with our fellows in a glowing exaltation of affection and make life in all its aspects seem not only worth living, but divinely beautiful and significant, and if this heavenly, world-transfiguring drug were of such a kind that we could wake up next morning with a clear head and an un-damaged constitution—then, it seems to me, all our problems (and not merely the one small problem of discovering a novel pleasure) would be wholly solved and earth would become paradise.

The nearest approach to such a new drug—and how im-measurably remote it is from the ideal intoxicant!—is the drug of speed. Speed, it seems to me, provides the one genuinely modern pleasure. True, men have always enjoyed speed; but their enjoyment has been limited, until very recent times, by the capacities of the horse, whose maximum velocity is not much more than thirty miles an hour. Now thirty miles an hour on a horse *feels* very much faster than sixty miles an hour in a train or a hundred in an aeroplane. The train is too large and steady, the aeroplane too remote from stationary surroundings, to give their passengers a very intense sensation of speed. The auto-mobile is sufficiently small and sufficiently near the ground to be able to compete, as an intoxicating speed-purveyor, with the galloping horse. The inebriating effects of speed are noticeable, on horseback, at about twenty miles an hour, in a car at about sixty. When the car has passed seventy-two, or thereabouts, one begins to feel an unprecedented sensation—a sensation which no man in the days of horses ever felt. It grows intenser with every increase of velocity. I myself have never travelled at much more than eighty miles an hour in a car; but those who have drunk a stronger brewage of this strange intoxicant tell me that new marvels await any one who has the opportunity of passing the hundred mark. At what point the pleasure turns into pain, I do not know. Long before the fantastic Daytona figures are reached, at any rate. Two hundred miles an hour must be absolute torture.

But in this, of course, speed is like all other pleasures; indulged in to excess, they become their opposites. Each particular pleasure has its corresponding particular pain, boredom, or disgust. The compensating drawback of too much speed-pleasure must be, I suppose, a horrible compound of intense physical discomfort and intense fear. No; if one must go in for excesses one would prob-ably be better advised to be old-fashioned and stick to overeating.

MIAHUATLAN

From *Beyond the Mexique Bay* (1934)

VICTORIAN England, outside the villages, the country houses and the genteeler quarters of the large towns, was a land of indescribable ugliness and misery. To escape from it, Karl Marx went out imaginatively into the revolutionary future, Ruskin and William Morris into the pre-industrial past.

Twentieth-century industrial America is not quite so obviously frightful as the nineteenth-century industrial England; moreover, its frightfulness was for some time concealed by a gaudy façade of success, behind which it was considered unpatriotic to peep. Some peeping, of course, there was; but the records of it, such as the Lynds' classical *Middletown*, made little popular appeal. Then, in 1929, with a loud and terrifying crash, the façade fell down. The ugliness stood revealed, and an ever-increasing sum of misery cried aloud to heaven. History has repeated itself. In their desire to escape from the horrors of industrial reality—to escape from, and at the same time to find a remedy for, them—some American thinkers have run forward into the revolutionary future; others, back into the pre-industrial past. But in Mexico the pre-industrial past still exists, is contemporary with the industrial depression across the border. The Ruskins and Morrises of modern New York do not have to use their imaginations to reconstruct the characteristics of a vanished way of life. They need only walk to the nearest Pan-American Airways office and buy a ticket. In a few hours they will find themselves in the midst of a fifteenth-century peasant society. Since the depression, books on Mexico have been almost as numerous, I should guess, as books on Russia. The Marxes flee Northwards, the Morrises towards the South.

Many of these books are marred by an injudicious extravagance of admiration for everything Mexican, or rather, for everything Indian in Mexico. This is only to be expected. The

Mexico of the Indians is more, for these writers, than a mere geographical and sociological reality; it is a place where wishes are fulfilled, and the intolerable evils of the civilized world corrected. Morris gave his contemporaries *News from Nowhere*; his successors give us news from Mexico. For critics of modern American society the Mexican Indians fulfil the functions reserved in the writings of Voltaire and his contemporaries to the Chinese and the Persians: they are alien cudgels for the beating of domestic malefactors. But whereas Voltaire never dreamed of actually visiting Peking, but was content to use his Chinamen as the disembodied symbols of a wisdom conspicuously absent from his own France, the Americans really take the train or the aeroplane and, having made the southern trip, are rash enough to affirm that their Noble Savages are genuine Mexican Indians.

The most judicious of the recent American books on Mexico is that of the well-known economist, Mr Stuart Chase. I had read it on its first appearance in 1932, and now, *en route*, with the realities of Central America before my eyes, read it again more critically and understandingly. It is worth while, I think, to discuss this book in some detail; for it attacks a problem which is surely of the first importance: the problem of reconciling the primitive with the civilized. Primitive societies have their characteristic virtues and their characteristic defects. The virtues of civilized societies are higher than those of primitive societies; but their defects are more enormous. (The corruption of the best is always the worst.) The question which confronts us is this: can we evolve a new society which shall combine the virtues of primitives with those of the civilized, but exhibit the vices of neither? Mr Chase poses this general question in a particular form: How much of what is good in North American civilization can Mexico import and still remain Mexico? His conclusion is that Mexico can, without danger, take over the following: modern hygiene *en bloc*; two or three million horse-power of electric energy for the grinding of corn, the refrigeration of food, and the general development of small-scale village industries;

and finally, some few thousand more miles of metalled roads with a sufficient number of new Fords to transport the burdens at present carried by patient armies of mules and asses, of men and women, of little boys and girls.

The intrinsic desirability of such importations is undeniable. But the question at once arises: Could the Mexicans introduce them and still retain the characteristics which Mr Chase finds so engaging? The answer is, pretty obviously, 'No'. Let us consider the effects, measured in purely human terms, of these importations. We will begin with the rules of hygiene. Incidentally, it seems very improbable that the Indians could be persuaded to accept these rules unless they had received a fairly elaborate preliminary education—an education which would already have made them rather, perhaps very, different from the Indians Mr Chase likes so much today. But let that pass. We will assume that the Indians have all gone hygienic. What are the results? An immediate and heavy decline in the infant mortality rate and an increase in the average expectation of life; consequently, within a few years, a rapid growth of population. But what happens when a population increases. Villages turn into towns and towns into cities. An urban and later, when cities have grown too large to be experienced as social unities, a suburban mentality is automatically brought into existence. The characteristic peasant virtues and defects cease to exist, and are replaced by the virtues and defects of townsmen. At the same time a heavy strain is thrown on the existing supply of food, clothing, shelter, and so forth. In order to meet the increased demand it becomes necessary to use scientific methods of agriculture and to mechanize the processes of manufacture. The electrically operated village industries may provide a sufficiency of cheap goods for this mounting population. Or they may not. It remains to be seen. In certain departments it may be that mass production will prove to be necessary. But even the rationalization of agriculture and the mechanization of village industries (without which, it is obvious, the new population must miserably starve) are profoundly disturbing processes, fatal to the old traditional ways of thinking and feeling. Men do not retain peasant psychologies when they have ceased to be peasants.

It may be argued that undue rise in the population can be prevented by judicious birth control. But again, you cannot teach primitive Indians to practise the neo-Malthusian techniques and expect them to remain primitive Indians.

'Character', says Mr J. H. Denison in that valuable, but as yet little known book, *Emotion as the Basis of Civilization*, 'character is formed by enforcing a system of taboos which causes men to feel a sense of horror for acts harmful to the community'—and, we may add, for acts only imagined to be harmful to the community. To change a society's taboo-system, even in part, is to change the character of its members, and along with their character the kind of emotions they feel and the kind of thoughts they think. It is unlikely, for example, that Indians brought up on Stopes would continue to celebrate *fiestas* in honour of the ancient fertility gods. But an Indian who has given up his *fiestas* would not be the simple-mindedly happy peasant beloved of Mr Chase.

And finally, there are the roads, the fleets of new Ford cars. What a huge intolerable load the Fords will lift from aching human backs! But the minds to which these backs belong—they will be changed. For, over and above their material freight, the Fords will carry an invisible cargo of new ideas, of alien, urban ways of thought and feeling. There are schools, now, in even the smallest villages. But their influence is still inconsiderable. For what, after all, is the good of knowing how to read in a place where no reading matter ever makes its appearance? Sometimes, it is true, a few scraps of print circulate in the far-off villages. But the stuff was written in the towns, by men with another philosophy of life. The village Indian can read; but his mind is so conditioned that he cannot understand what he reads. Along the metalled roads the Fords will bring, not only reading matter, but also notions that will make the printed words fully comprehensible. Education can be as platonic as love—ardent but discarnate and sterile. School in Mexico is Dante, and the

Indian mind has remained up till now barrenly Beatrice. Roads and motor cars will give to Mexican education a new potency. The untouched, untouchable Beatrice will conceive, bring forth. Backed up by the Fords, the village schools will at last begin to do what they were meant to do—transform the national character. And then good-bye—yet once more—to Mr Chase's Indians. The more sensitive among us abhor the noisy restless vulgarity of our urban civilization; we envy the primitive his serene, self-sufficing contentment. But the primitive is fascinated by the very things we dislike. For example, Indians were taken from the wilds to be given a course of instruction at a training centre in Mexico City. The idea was that, when they had passed their examinations, they should return as school-masters to their villages. But the great majority refused to return; they preferred to become wage-slaves in the festering slums of the metropolis. It has been decided now to train village teachers in the provincial towns. Less vulgarly 'modern' than the capital, they will, it is hoped, exercise a less powerful attraction. The metalled roads and the Fords will have the effect of making large-scale urban vulgarity accessible to almost all. And wherever urban vulgarity is made accessible to primitives they rush headlong to embrace it. This dismal truth is confirmed by daily examples from every corner of the world.

From all this one conclusion evidently emerges: Mr Chase's programme is unworkable. You cannot import North American virtues and North American amenities into Mexico without causing the Mexicans to lose their Mexican virtues and to abandon what is best in their own Mexican way of life.

Must we then despair of this most desirable consummation— the wedding of primitive with civilized virtues? I think not. Partially to industrialize and civilize primitives may be impossible. But to introduce a salutary element of primitivism into our civilized and industrialized way of life—this, I believe, can be done. The undeveloped consciousness of the primitive leaves him at the mercy of influences coming from civilization. Lacking a critical faculty, he is unable to take only the good and reject the rest. With him it is all or nothing; he must accept everything that comes his way. But, for us, the case is different. A critical faculty has been developed, at any rate in the more intelligent members of every civilized community. Where primitives accept the world, society, tradition, unquestioningly, as fishes accept the water in which they swim, the civilized are able to stand back from their mental and material surroundings, to pass judgment upon them. It is possible for them to realize what is wrong with their own way of thinking and feeling and to appreciate all that is desirable in the primitive form of life.

It is easy to draw up a list of these desirable elements in the patterns of primitive existence; difficult to say how many of these elements could possibly be incorporated into the pattern of civilization. Many primitive virtues are obviously incompatible with urbanism and industrialism (both to a great extent unavoidable, where population is dense), with individual self-consciousness, with education in scientific method, and with a high level of material prosperity. For example, the extreme stability of primitive communities is unattainable in our large heterogeneous societies, composed of individuals who have ceased to believe in the supernatural sanctions of traditional taboos. Nor can we expect people at a certain level of education to be content with the extreme simplicities of primitive life; nor that, possessed of enough self-consciousness to make originality seem desirable and of enough material resources to make the expression of personality an easy matter, they should always observe the negative good taste of peasants who unquestioningly accept an old tradition and who lack the means to make more than a very small splash. Vulgarity is largely a matter of opportunity; when people are given a chance to be vulgar, they generally are vulgar. Civilized people have many opportunities, and take them—alas, on what an enormous scale!

So much for what civilized men cannot take from their primitive neighbours. What *can* they take? They can take, or at least they can try to take the primitive's human wholeness. A primitive is forced to be whole—a complete man, trained in all the skills of the community, able to fend for himself in all circumstances; if he is not whole, he perishes. A civilized man, on the contrary, is under no external necessity to be whole. He can go comfortably and, as we judge success, successfully through life, incapable of doing anything except, shall we say, writing detective novels; within the strong economic and legal framework of civilization he is perfectly safe. A highly organized society protects him from the worst effects of his own incompetence; allows him to be ignorant of all the useful arts and yet to live. So far as immediate physical disaster is concerned, he can be unwhole with impunity. But there are also psychological disasters—the gradual disasters of atrophy and decay. Our admirably efficient organization has no power to save a man from these. Indeed its very perfection is the cause of these individual disasters. All civilization, and especially industrial civilization, tends to turn human beings into the mere embodiments of particular social functions. The community gains in efficiency; but the individual is maimed.

Man's biological success was due to the fact that he never specialized. Unfitted by his physique to do any one thing to perfection, he was forced to develop the means for doing everything reasonably well. Civilization reverses the evolutionary process. Generalized by nature, we impose upon ourselves, artificially, the narrowest specializations. Primitives are men who have never succumbed to the suicidal ambition to resemble ants. Generalization—this is the great, the vitally important lesson they have to teach the specialists of the civilized world. The problem is to evolve a society that shall retain all or most of the material and intellectual advantages resulting from specialization, while allowing its members to lead to the full the life of generalized human beings. To solve this problem will be hard, but not, I am convinced, impossible.

OAXACA

From *Beyond the Mexique Bay* (1934)

POTTERY, *sarape* weaving, leather-work, the ornamental plaiting of string, and the making of *machetes* and swords—these are the principal local handicrafts. The last seems to be mainly a white man's and mestizo's industry. The other crafts are purely Indian and are practised in the outlying villages as well as in the town itself. The leather-work is poor; but the pots are pleasant and the gaily coloured string bags and haversacks very pretty, in a rather childish way. Of the *sarapes*, some are quietly unpretentious—dark blankets with a minimum of pattern in grey or white on a black ground. But there are also more ambitious designs. One finds, for example, a lamb or a Mexican eagle, carried out in white, black and grey, with touches of red and green. Sometimes letters will be woven into the picture—a *Viva Mexico*, for example. A few of these blankets are excellent; the rest are dull and sometimes downright ugly. This is only to be expected; for the more ambitious the design, the greater scope for individual talent and the more narrowly restricted the influence of tradition. But individual talent is rare; correspondingly rare, it follows, must be the designs whose excellence depends upon it.

Much nonsense has recently been talked about Indian handicrafts. Fleeing from the slump and with the hideous vision of Zenith and Middletown still painfully fresh in their memories, the new William Morrises from the United States have come to Mexico and, confronted by its peasant arts, have broken out into an intemperate and hysterical enthusiasm. Middletown and Zenith are nightmarish; but this is no reason for asserting that the pretty little peasantries of the Mexican Indians are intrinsically significant works of art. Peasant art is hardly ever intrinsically significant as art; its value is social and psychological, not aesthetic. Mr Chase says of a well-known arts-and-crafts shop

in Mexico City that it is 'as exciting to him as any art museum.'
If that is so, then either Mr Chase is wholly without a feeling
for aesthetic values, or else he is mistaking for aesthetic excitement the pleasure which he derives, as a sociologist, from the
mere idea of craftsmanship. The wage-slaves of Middletown
spend their days alternately working at machines and being
passively amused by machines. The craftsmen of Mexico simultaneously work and play at making pots and blankets, lacquer
bowls and the like. The wage-slave's life is restless and un-
satisfying; the craftsman's life (at any rate in many cases) is
serene and satisfying. Moreover, the craftsman is unaffected by
slumps; the wage-slave periodically starves. Pots, blankets,
lacquer, are the symbols of the Mexican craftsman's safer and
more wholesome life. In the presence of these symbols, Mr
Chase, the sociologist, feels excited, and, through a roseate fog
of mental confusion, the excitement communicates itself to
Mr Chase, the aesthete. This is, I think, the most plausible, as
it is certainly the most charitable, explanation of Mr Chase's
remark. For, if he really finds a collection of peasant bric-à-brac
as exciting as an art museum—*any* art museum, mark you: the
Prado, for example, the National Gallery—well, then, heaven
help him! For he is a man to whom nature has denied all sense
of the qualitative difference between things.

The whole subject of folk-art is in a state of great confusion
and urgently demands to be clarified. Like Mr Chase, most
enthusiasts for handicrafts tend to attribute too much aesthetic
merit to the result of activities whose real value is psychological
social and economic. It is good that large numbers of people
should be craftsmen, not because there is the smallest prospect of
their producing a correspondingly large number of good works
of art, but because craftsmanship is something which most men
and women find psychologically satisfying. I myself, for example,
spend much of my spare time painting pictures. The exercise of
this manual skill gives me extraordinary pleasure; but I do not
for that reason imagine that I am producing masterpieces. So far
as the ordinary untalented, or slightly talented, individual is con-

cerned, craftsmanship is its own reward. And because it is its own reward, it is also socially useful. Craftsmanship brings psychological fulfilment; a society of craftsmen is a society of satisfied individuals; and a society of satisfied individuals tends to be a stable society. Craftsmanship has a further social utility, inasmuch as an economy based upon handwork is less alarmingly liable to fluctuation than one whose foundation is mass production. Thus we see that, even if all craft-work and peasant art were uniformly hideous, craftsmanship would still be of the highest value. In point of fact, craft-work is never uniformly hideous. In their own way, the production of a people of handicraftsmen are often excellent; but the nature of this excellence is essentially inferior to that of the excellence we find in the work of a great artist.

The life of an epoch is expressed by, and at the same time is itself an expression of, the art of that epoch. Where popular art is vulgar, there the life of the people is also essentially vulgar in its emotional quality. The popular arts in our industrialized communities are of an unprecedented vulgarity. Why should this be? And what is the precise nature of this vulgarity? What, again, is the nature of the relative refinement of the popular folk-arts of peasants and craftsmen?

The nature of contemporary vulgarity has been well illustrated and analysed by Mr Leavis and Mr Denys Thompson in their book *Culture and Environment*. So far as it goes, it is an excellent little book. Its great defect is that it does not go far enough. For its authors are content merely to describe the symptoms of the disease and to suggest an educational treatment to combat them. But it is not by palliating symptoms that you can effect a real cure. Rational treatment must be based on a knowledge of the deep-rooted causes of the disease. Mr Leavis and Mr Thompson are like clinicians who should carefully describe the fever and the pustules, without ever mentioning the virus which is the cause of these symptoms of smallpox. This is the principal defect of their book. Another, less serious, but still grave, is their extremely uncritical assumption that the arts of pre-industrial civilization were not merely relatively refined, but always absolutely excellent. At the end of the book we find a series of questions, intended for the use of teachers. One of these is worded as follows: 'Do you know of any ugly building, furniture, tools, etc., before 1820? Account, as far as you can, for your findings.' The context makes it clear that one is supposed to answer this question in the negative. One is supposed never to have seen any ugly building, furniture or tools of a date anterior to 1820. And, of course, if one is an uncritical archaeolater, one never does see any ugliness in the productions of earlier civilizations. But for any sensitive and unprejudiced person, a walk through any museum of decorative art, through any old town, brings instant proof that the pre-industrial age was rich in all manner of ugliness and ineptitude.

The truth is, of course, that most art has always been either bad or indifferent. This is inevitable. Artistic talent is an extremely rare phenomenon; therefore good art is extremely uncommon. The only substitute—and it is at best a partial substitute—for personal talent is a good artistic tradition. This enables people with little talent to produce good work because it relieves them of the necessity for using their own second-rate, or tenth-rate, imaginations. A good tradition may be defined as the ghosts of good dead artists dictating to bad living artists. So long as the bad artists listen to the dictations, and so long as they make no attempt to launch out on their own account, they will produce good derivative work. But an artistic tradition need not necessarily be good. For generations the ghosts of bad artists may dictate to other bad artists; the results, when that happens, are deplorable. But even at its worst the bad art of pre-industrial times is seldom quite so depressing and never so painfully vulgar as modern bad art.

The badness and vulgarity of modern popular art are the result of a number of interlocking causes. The most important of these are the increase of population; the improvement of old techniques for treating raw materials and the invention of new ones; the rise of the standards of living; and finally, the development within the arts themselves of new and more powerful modes of expression. Let us deal with these in order.

The enormous increase of population during the last century is due to several causes. The cultivation of virgin soil in the New World and the introduction of Chilean nitrates into the Old, suddenly quintupled the world's available food supply. Power production made it possible to provide clothing and shelter for indefinite millions of new people. At the same time public hygiene reduced infantile mortality and raised the average age of death. Most of the new millions thus called into being collected in the towns, which were thus swollen to unprecedented dimensions. Now, it seems to me very doubtful whether it is mechanically possible for a very large city to be anything but ugly and depressing. Give to London all the town planning, all the civic centres, all the garden suburbs that the ingenuity of man can devise; it will still remain an assemblage of a million houses sprawling over five or six hundred square miles of ground. And even if every one of these million houses were a masterpiece of architecture (which is humanly impossible), the total effect of their agglomeration would still be profoundly depressing. Avila is a city of extraordinary beauty; but magnify it five or six hundred times, so as to make it as large as London, and Avila will be hideous, a place of interminable monotonies, of hopeless dreariness and suffocating oppression. All our great cities could do with an immense amount of improvement. But we must not flatter ourselves with the belief that these improvements will transform them into things of beauty. Only a ninety-per-cent. destruction can accomplish that miracle.

Undue increase of city population has a psychological effect which I can best sum up by saying that all urbanization, pushed beyond a certain point, automatically becomes suburbanization. The inhabitants of a small city can take part in all its activities; they are able to experience their native place as a single living unit. A large city cannot be experientially known; its life is too manifold for any individual to be able to participate in it. Every great city is just a collection of suburbs. Its inhabitants have lost the advantages of living in the country without acquiring the compensating advantages of living in a town. For they do not *live* in their city; they merely inhabit it. Their minds are neither rustic nor urban, but suburban; and experience seems to show that a suburban mind is not a soil in which good traditions of art easily flourish.

The mechanization of industry has deprived millions of people of the opportunity to practise a handicraft, and by so doing has destroyed many excellent traditions of applied art. Mr Leavis and Mr Thompson have expatiated at some length on this obvious point. But mechanization has had another and no less disastrous effect on the popular arts. The general improvement of technical processes has helped to bring about the general deterioration of taste. We pray that we may not be led into temptation; and with good reason. For it is opportunity that makes most of the murderers, the thieves, the adulterers. Opportunity, too, that makes most of the vulgarians. One fact emerges clearly from the history of art: that whenever men have had the means to be vulgar, they have generally succumbed to the temptation and made use of them.

Vulgarity is always the result of some excess; and the means to vulgarity are therefore means to the realization in practice of an inward tendency toward the excessive. These means to vulgarity are of two kinds, economic and technical. You cannot achieve excess, and therefore vulgarity, unless, first, you have enough money to undertake personally, or to buy from others, works of art on a considerable scale, and, second, unless you or your employees are equipped with enough technical ability to make possible the artistic expression of your inward urge towards excess.

Before discussing the technical means to vulgarity, it will be as well to say a few words about the economic conditions for its realization in terms of art. 'It pays to advertise' is a maxim as old as civilization. The rich and eminent members of every society have always spent a certain proportion of their incomes on display. They have paid copy-writers and poster-designers to 'put them across' in nation-wide publicity drives. Sometimes these copy-writers were called Vergil or Spenser, these poster-designers, Holbein or Velasquez or Tiepolo. But often the ruler's or the rich man's desire for publicity has been gratified by artists of inferior quality. Hence, from the tomb of Tutank-hamen to the Queen Victoria Memorial, those innumerable monuments of vulgarity which constitute, in such large measure, what is beautifully called the World's Artistic Heritage.

Folk-art is often dull or insignificant; never vulgar, and for an obvious reason. Peasants lack, first, the money, and, second, the technical skill to achieve those excesses which are the essence of vulgarity. Vulgarity has always been the privilege of the prosperous and the highly educated. The general rise in the standard of living has meant a general increase in vulgarity. For the first time in the world's history the small bourgeoisie and even a part of the proletariat have been able to treat them-selves to the luxuries previously reserved to members of the ruling class. Conspicuous among these luxuries is artistic vulgarity.

So much for the economic means to vulgarity. The technical means are of two kinds—those concerned primarily with the treatment of matter and those concerned primarily with the treatment of the invisible entities in a work of art: ideas and emotions.

Wherever artists find much technical difficulty in imposing form on brute matter, art tends to be simple, severe and chaste. It cannot be anything else. Luxuriance, unchastity and conse-quent vulgarity become possible only when men have acquired almost complete mastery over matter. It is when they can express themselves freely that artists begin to reveal their true character. The man of delicate and noble talent will express freely his delicacy and nobility; the man whose talent is coarse and vulgar will be able at last to give free rein to his coarseness and vulgarity. This is why any improvement in the techniques of subduing matter to spirit is always attended by an increase in vulgarity. Only an artist of exceptional austerity can make a temperate use of the resources of a highly developed technology. Significantly enough, many sensitive artists of this age have adopted towards modern technique an attitude analogous to that of a hermit towards the pleasure of the world. Fearful of temptation, they retire into the desert—an artificial desert of their own making, a little oasis of technical aridity in the midst of the prevailing luxuriance. They are perhaps wise. Personally, however, I should have admired them more if they had faced the problem a little more courageously—gone out into the luxuriance and tried to master it. But that is by the way.

Advances in technology have led not only to vulgarity, but also, indirectly, to the lowering of qualitative standards in all the popular arts. Process reproduction and the rotary press have made possible the indefinite multiplication of writing and pictures. Universal education and relatively high wages have created an enormous public who know how to read and can afford to buy reading matter and pictorial seeing matter. A great industry has been called into existence in order to supply these commodities. Now, artistic talent is a very rare phenomenon; whence it follows (as I have already remarked) that, at every epoch and in all countries, most art has been bad. But the proportion of trash in the total artistic output is greater now than at any other period. That it must be so is a matter of simple arithmetic. The population of Western Europe has a little more than doubled during the last century. But the amount of reading- and seeing-matter has increased, I should imagine, at least twenty and possibly fifty or even a hundred times. If there were n men of talent in a population of x millions, there will presumably be $2n$ men of talent among $2x$ millions. The situation may be summed up thus. For every page of print and pictures published a century ago, twenty, or perhaps even a hundred pages are published today. But for every man of talent then living, there are now only two men of talent. It may be of course that, thanks to universal education, many potential talents which in the past would have been still-born are now enabled to realize themselves. Let us assume, then, that there are now three or even four men of talent to every one of earlier times. It still remains true to say that the consumption of reading- and seeing-matter has far outstripped the natural production of gifted writers and draughtsmen. It is the same with hearing-matter. Prosperity, the gramophone and the radio have created an audience of hearers who consume an amount of hearing-matter that has increased out of all proportion to the increase of population and the consequent natural increase of talented musicians. It follows from all this that in all the arts the output of trash is both absolutely and relatively greater than it was in the past; and that it must remain greater for just so long as the world continues to consume the present inordinate quantities of reading-matter, seeing-matter and hearing-matter.

So far I have spoken only of technical improvements in the handling of materials. There have also been purely aesthetic advances in the technique of expression. Of these the most startling are to be found in the domain of music. Beethoven made it possible to give direct and poignant expression to a great number of thoughts and feelings, which owing to the absence of a suitable idiom, were inexpressible by even the most highly gifted of his predecessors. Beethoven's aesthetic discoveries were exploited by other men in order to express thoughts and feelings of greatly inferior quality. The same thing happened in the case of all the great musical innovators of the nineteenth and early twentieth centuries. Thanks to Beethoven, to Berlioz, to Wagner (himself a sad vulgarian) to Rimsky-Korsakov, to Debussy, to Stravinsky, the modern jazz composer is in a position to express (with what an appalling technical efficiency!) every shade of all the baser emotions, from a baboon-like lust to a nauseating self-commiseration, from the mindless mass hysteria of howling mobs to a languishing masturbatory *Träumerei*. The first popular waltz, as I pointed out some years ago, was *Ach, du lieber Augustin*. Compare that innocently silly little tune with a successful waltz or blues of today. The distance travelled has been enormous. Towards what goal? One shudders to imagine it. And the joke, the atrocious and deplorable joke, is that this

Gadarene progress has been made possible by the labours of some of the most noble and delicate spirits known to history.

What is the upshot of it all? So far as I can see, it is this: that the vulgarity which characterizes our industrial civilization is part of the inevitable result or concomitant of our prosperity, our universal instruction, our technological progress, our urbanization. Mr Leavis and Mr Thompson seem to think that the remedy for vulgarity and the general lowering of qualitative standards lies in better education; and certainly something can be done by teaching such children as are teachable to distinguish between the good and the bad, the bogus and the genuine. But I doubt whether education can restore us to complete emotional and artistic health. The psychological, social and economic forces now making towards vulgarization, are too strong to be resisted by a handful of school teachers (themselves, incidentally, more or less seriously infected by the disease they are supposed to cure). A change in the existing organization of society might do some good. For example, it might be possible, while preserving the advantages of machine production, to reintroduce, to some extent, the practice of handicrafts. Freed from the burden of competition, the organizers of industry could afford to create and artificially preserve little Red Indian Reservations of craftsmanship in the midst of a world of machines. Again, the state could train its citizens for a leisure in which the practice of handicrafts should play an important part. That love of 'hobbies', so common in every class of society, could be systematized, could be given a new, more dignified status, a higher social significance. The psychological effects of such a policy would probably be excellent. But it does not follow that, because a man is contented, he will produce good art. I see no reason to suppose that the arts and crafts of a prosperous, technically efficient and relatively well-educated society would possess even the negative virtues of peasant art. For these negative virtues, as I have already shown, are the result of poverty and ignorance. A society of civilized handicraftsmen could never blindly accept an old tradition. There would always be attempts at originality—attempts foredoomed, in the great majority of cases, to failure; for only highly talented artists can hope to be original with success. The partial restoration of handicraft culture would probably make for personal happiness and social stability, but would do little, so far as I can see, to cure vulgarity. Vulgarity is the price we must pay for prosperity, education and self-consciousness. Nor must we forget the influence of quantity upon quality. So long as population remains at its present density, ugliness is inevitable. For, reduplicated a million times, even the most beautiful object becomes hideous. Even more hideous will seem the endless repetitions of objects originally and intrinsically ugly. And intrinsically ugly they must be; for, in a large, prosperous, and educated population, it is impossible that the level of popular art should be high. It is impossible because, as I have shown, the consumption of the arts has increased far more rapidly than the natural production of men of talent. Great quantity inevitably creates bad quality and multiplies it till it becomes a nightmare.

So far, then, as the popular arts are concerned, the prospect is none too good. Perhaps the wisest thing to do is to abandon them to their inevitable vulgarity and ineptitude and to concentrate all available resources on the training of a minority that shall be capable of appreciating the higher activities of the spirit. *Il faut cultiver notre oasis.*

T. H. HUXLEY AS A LITERARY MAN[1]

From *The Olive Tree* (1936) (*an extract*)

THE function of language is twofold: to communicate emotion and to give information. The rudimentary language of the lower animals seems to be purely emotive. Beasts make noises to express desire, fear, anger and the like; to let off their superfluous energy; and to make their presence known to their fellow-creatures. Never do they express a concept. When a startled blackbird fles off at our approach with his characteristic cry, he is not saying, 'There is a man'; he is saying, 'I am afraid' —or rather, he is simply screaming with terror. And at the sound of the scream, other blackbirds are terrified. Communication is by emotional infection, never, apparently, by conceptual statement.

Man has invented concepts. He does not merely scream with terror: he also says why and of what he is afraid. The noises he makes stand for classes of objects. He can do what the animal can never do: he can make an exact statement untinged by passion. In other words, he can write scientifically.

But because he *can* do this, it does not follow that he very often wants to do it. In most of the circumstances of life, he wants not only to inform, but also to move—above all, to be moved as well as to be informed. Literature is the art of making statements movingly.

Now, the emotions which a literary statement may cause us to feel are of two distinct types. They may be what I will call the 'biological emotions'—emotions, that is to say, with a survival value, such as fear, anger, delight or disgust, all of which we share with the lower animals. Or they may be more specifically human emotions—luxury feelings, which we might lose without seriously imperilling our chances of survival.

Literature, in common with the other arts, arouses in us, over

[1] Part of the Huxley Memorial Lecture 1932.

and above any kind of biological emotion, a certain luxury feel-ing, to which we give the name of the aesthetic emotion. We describe as beautiful anything which makes us experience this feeling.

Let us now consider the case of a writer who is trying to make a statement which shall cause his readers to have a certain bio-logical feeling—say, a feeling of anger. By using words with suitable significances and associations, by expressing himself in terms of metaphors that call up the right kind of images, he can make it clear to his readers that he feels angry himself (or, vicariously, in the person of a fictional character) and that he wants them to feel angry too. Whether they respond or remain unmoved depends, to a very considerable extent, on his powers as an artist—on his powers, that is to say, as a giver of aesthetic emotions. If he can arrange his words and phrases in a pattern which his readers will consider beautiful, then he is likely to succeed. If not, he is likely to fail. Biological feelings can be well and promptly communicated only by words arranged so as to give us aesthetic feelings. And the same thing is true even of the most abstract ideas. We are more likely to take in an idea which is expressed with art, beautifully, than if it is expressed in language that gives us no aesthetic satisfaction.

True, facts and theories *can* be communicated in terms that give the reader no aesthetic satisfaction. So can the passions. But neither passion nor facts and theories can be communicated rapidly and persuasively in such terms. Whatever is expressed with art—whether it be a lover's despair or a metaphysical theory—pierces the mind and compels assent and acceptance. Against that which is expressed without art, our understandings are naturally armoured. We have a certain difficulty in taking in anything that is not intrinsically elegant; a certain eagerness to accept anything that moves us aesthetically. Handsome faces are sometimes associated with ugly characters; and in the same way, alas! literary art may be associated with untruth. The natural human tendency to believe what is beautiful has been the source of innumerable errors. If only Plato had written as badly as Immanuel Kant! But his voice was, unfortunately, the voice of an angel, even when it was uttering demonstrable nonsense. And if Darwin's style had been as excellent as Samuel Butler's, Mr Bernard Shaw would not at present be a preacher of Lamarckism—'a doctrine', as Professor J. B. S. Haldane has remarked, 'supported by far less positive evidence than exists for the reality of witchcraft'.

Science is investigation. But if it were only investigation, it would be without fruit, and useless. Henry Cavendish investigated for the mere fun of the thing, and left the world in ignorance of his most important discoveries. Our admiration for his genius is tempered by a certain disapproval; we feel that such a man is selfish and anti-social. Science is investigation; yes. But it is also, and no less essentially, communication. But all communication is literature. In one of its aspects, then, science is a branch of literature.

It may be objected that I apply the term 'literature' too indiscriminately—that, instead of using the word to cover all verbal communications whatsoever, I should limit its connotation to a certain class of communications. To this objection, I reply interrogatively: Which particular class of verbal communications constitutes literature? The answers to this question are generally very vague. For example, literature has been defined as 'the interpretation of life through the medium of words'; while a distinction is often drawn between 'words used to record observations of fact, either as an end in themselves, or as a basis for generalizations, and words used as a means for transferring experience'. But, frankly, this sort of thing won't do; it is too hazy. Not much better is the distinction between literature and science implied by Wordsworth in his preface to the *Lyrical Ballads*. 'The remotest discoveries of the chemist, the botanist, or the mineralogist will be as proper objects of the poet's art as any upon which he is now employed, if the time should ever come, when these things shall be familiar to us, and the relations under which they are contemplated shall be manifestly and palpably material to us as enjoying and suffering beings.' But who, we may inquire, are the people whom Words-worth calls 'us'? Is it not obvious that the more intelligent a man is, and the more highly cultivated, the wider will be the range of things which are 'material to him as an enjoying and suffering being'? Moreover, as every verbal communication can be made well or badly, every verbal communication is susceptible of affect-ing some men, at any rate, as aesthetic enjoyers and sufferers. It goes without saying, of course, that only those who under-stand the terms in which the communication is made will have any aesthetic feelings about it. Englishmen are clearly not the best judges of Chinese poetry, and those who have not had a scientific education will be unable to understand, much less to appreciate and enjoy, works written in a highly technical language. But for anyone who knows what they are talking about, the very mathematicians are men of letters—men of algebraical letters, no doubt; but even x and $sigma$ and psi can be aesthetically good or bad, *litterae humaniores* or inhuman letters. I have heard mathematicians groaning over the demonstrations of Kelvin. Ponderous and clumsy, they bludgeon the mind into a reluctant assent. Whereas to be convinced by Clerk Maxwell's elegant equations is a pleasure; and reading Niels Abel on hyper-elliptic functions is almost, it seems, like listening to Mozart's chamber music. For the mathematically illiterate, like myself, these things are, of course, mere scribblings, without significance and without form. For those whom Nature has endowed with suitable talents and who have had the right education, they are works of art, some exquisite, some atrociously bad. What is true of a mathematical argument is equally true of arguments couched in words. Even plain records of observed fact may be, in their own way, beautiful or ugly. From all which we must conclude that all verbal communications whatsoever are literature.

Some kinds of literature, however, are more widely accessible than others. Also, certain classes of experience give more artistic scope to those who communicate them than do certain other classes of experience. For example, a man who writes about his experiences of love or pain has more scope for arranging words in an aesthetically satisfying way than one who sets out to give an account of his observations on, say, deep-sea fish. All communications are literature; but their potentialities for beauty are unequal. A good account of deep-sea fish can never be as richly, variously and subtly beautiful as a good poem about love. But, on the other hand, a bad account of fish can probably never be so monstrous as a bad love-poem.

To make clearer what I have been saying, let me give two specific examples. The following is an extract from an article in the *Encyclopaedia Britannica* on the furnishing of Anglican churches after the Reformation: 'When tables were substituted for altars in the English churches, these were not merely movable, but, at the administration of the Lord's Supper, were actually moved into the body of the church, and placed *table-wise*—that is, with the long sides turned to the north and south, and the narrow ends to the east and west. In the time of Archbishop Laud, however, the present practice of the Church of England was introduced. The communion table, though still of wood and movable, is, in fact, never moved; it is placed *altar-wise*—that is, with the longer axis running north and south. Often there is a reredos behind it; it is also fenced in by rails to preserve it from profanation of various kinds.'

This is a simple and, as it happens, not a very good specimen of scientific literature. We read it without feeling any emotion, whether biological or aesthetic. The words are neither exciting nor beautiful; they are merely informative—and informative in what is, on the whole, rather an inelegant way.

Let us now listen to what Milton had to say on the same subject. 'The table of communion, now becomes a table of separation, stands like an exalted platform on the brow of the quire, fortified with bulwark and barricado to keep off the profane touch of the laics, whilst the obscene and surfeited priest scruples not to paw and mammock the sacramental bread as familiarly as his tavern biscuit.'

This is a statement about church furnishing; but not, as I think you may have noticed, a scientific statement—that is to say, a merely informative and unimpassioned statement. Milton, it is clear, designed to communicate, along with the facts about altars, certain biological feelings of his own—as hatred of priests and sympathy for an exploited laity. Thanks to the skilful use of a number of technical literary devices—devices which, unfortunately, I have no time to describe and analyse—the passage also gives us a lively feeling of aesthetic satisfaction. Milton communicates what he has to say with art; that is to say, he communicates it successfully. He really makes us feel, at any rate while we are reading him, some of his own indignation.

Huxley, as I shall show in due course, was an artist in both these kinds of literature—an artist in pure scientific statement, and also, on occasion, an artist in the communication of what I have called the biological feelings. Both his pure scientific and his emotive statements arouse aesthetic feelings; in other words, each kind of statement is, in its own way, beautiful.

Huxley realized very well the importance of being an artist. Of the Germans he writes: 'As men of research in positive science they are magnificently laborious and accurate. But most of them have no notion of style, and seem to compose their books with a pitchfork.' Determined that his own books should not justify a similar reproach, he cultivated his literary gifts with conscientious industry. 'It constantly becomes more and more difficult for me to *finish* things satisfactorily,' he writes to Hooker in 1860. The reason for this was that his standard of literary excellence was constantly becoming higher. Let me quote in this context a letter to his French translator, de Varigny. 'I am quite conscious that the condensed and idiomatic English into which I always try to put my thoughts must present many difficulties to a translator. . . . The fact is that I have a great love and respect for my native tongue, and take great pains to use it properly. Sometimes I write essays half a dozen times before I can get them into the proper shape; and I believe I become more fastidious as I grow older.' It was an effective fastidiousness; Huxley undoubtedly wrote better as he grew older.

What were his artistic principles and ideals? The following

passage from a letter to the *Pall Mall Gazette* in 1886 is illuminating:

'That a young Englishman may be turned out of one of our universities, "epopt and perfect", as far as their system takes him, and yet ignorant of the noble literature which has grown up in these islands during the last three centuries, no less than of the philosophical and political ideas which have most profoundly influenced modern civilization, is a fact in the history of the nineteenth century which the twentieth will find hard to believe; though perhaps it is not more incredible than our current superstition that who so wishes to write and speak English well should mould his style after the models furnished by classical antiquity. For my part, I venture to doubt the wisdom of attempting to mould one's style by any other process than that of striving after the clear and forcible expression of definite conceptions; in which process the Glassian precept, "first catch your definite conceptions", is probably the most difficult to obey. But still I mark among distinguished contemporary speakers and writers of English, saturated with antiquity, not a few to whom, it seems to me, the study of Hobbes might have taught dignity, of Swift, concision and clearness, of Goldsmith and Defoe, simplicity.

'Well, among a hundred young men whose university career is finished, is there one whose attention has ever been directed by his literary instructors to a page of Hobbes, or Swift, or Goldsmith, or Defoe? In my boyhood we were familiar with *Robinson Crusoe, The Vicar of Wakefield* and *Gulliver's Travels*; and though the treasures of "Middle English" were hidden from us, my impression is that we ran less chance of learning to write and speak the "middling English" of popular orators and head masters than if we had been perfect in such mysteries and ignorant of those three masterpieces. It has been the fashion to decry the eighteenth century, as young fops laugh at their fathers. But we were there in germ; and a "Professor of Eighteenth-Century

History and Literature" who knew his business might tell young Englishmen more of that which it is profoundly important that they should know, but which at present remains hidden from them, than any other instructor: and, incidentally, they would learn to know good English when they see or hear it—perhaps even to distinguish between slipshod copiousness and true eloquence, and that alone would be a great gain.'

To literary beginners, Huxley's advice was: 'Say that which has to be said in such language that you can stand cross-examination on each word.' And again: 'Be clear, though you may be convicted of error. If you are clearly wrong, you will run up against a fact sometime and get set right. If you shuffle with your subject and study chiefly to use language which will give you a loophole of escape either way, there is no hope for you.' 'Veracity', he said on another occasion, 'is the heart of morality'. It was also the heart of his literary style. For all those rhetorical devices by means of which the sophist and the politician seek to make the worse appear the better cause Huxley felt an almost passionate disapproval. 'When some chieftain,' he wrote, 'famous in political warfare, ventures into the region of letters or of science, in full confidence that the methods which have brought fame and honour in his own province will answer there, he is apt to forget that he will be judged by those people on whom rhetorical artifices have long since ceased to take effect; and to whom mere dexterity in putting together cleverly ambiguous phrases, and even the great art of offensive misrepresentation, are unspeakably wearisome.'

The chieftain in question was Mr Gladstone, with whom, in 1891, Huxley was having the Gadarene swine controversy. Four years later, in the last year of his life, Huxley was to remark, in a conversation recorded by Mr Wilfrid Ward, on the philosophical methods of another eminent politician, Mr Arthur Balfour. 'No human being holds the opinion he (Balfour) speaks of as Naturalism. He is a good debater. He knows the value of a word. The word "Naturalism" has a bad sound and unpleasant associations. It would tell against us in the House of Commons, and so it will with his readers.' Huxley was also a good debater; he also knew the value of a word. But his passion for veracity always kept him from taking any unfair rhetorical advantages of an opponent. The candour with which he acknowledged a weakness in his own case was always complete, and though he made full use of a rich variety of literary devices to bring home what he wanted to say, he never abused his great rhetorical powers. Truth was more important to him than personal triumph, and he relied more on a forceful clarity to convince his readers than on the brilliant and exciting ambiguities of propagandist eloquence.

TIME AND THE MACHINE

From *The Olive Tree* (1936)

TIME, as we know it, is a very recent invention. The modern time-sense is hardly older than the United States. It is a by-product of industrialism—a sort of psychological analogue of synthetic perfumes and aniline dyes.

Time is our tyrant. We are chronically aware of the moving minute hand, even of the moving second hand. We have to be. There are trains to be caught, clocks to be punched, tasks to be done in specified periods, records to be broken by fractions of a second, machines that set the pace and have to be kept up with. Our consciousness of the smallest units of time is now acute. To us, for example, the moment 8.17 A.M. means something— something very important, if it happens to be the starting time of our daily train. To our ancestors, such an odd eccentric instant was without significance—did not even exist. In inventing the locomotive, Watt and Stephenson were part inventors of time.

Another time-emphasizing entity is the factory and its dependent, the office. Factories exist for the purpose of getting certain quantities of goods made in a certain time. The old artisan worked as it suited him; with the result that consumers generally had to wait for the goods they had ordered from him. The factory is a device for making workmen hurry. The machine revolves so often each minute; so many movements have to be made, so many pieces produced each hour. Result: the factory worker (and the same is true, *mutatis mutandis*, of the office worker) is compelled to know time in its smallest fractions. In the hand-work age there was no such compulsion to be aware of minutes and seconds.

Our awareness of time has reached such a pitch of intensity that we suffer acutely whenever our travels take us into some corner of the world where people are not interested in minutes and seconds. The unpunctuality of the Orient, for example, is appalling to those who come freshly from a land of fixed meal-times and regular train services. For a modern American or Englishman, waiting is a psychological torture. An Indian accepts the blank hours with resignation, even with satisfaction. He has not lost the fine art of doing nothing. Our notion of time as a collection of minutes, each of which must be filled with some business or amusement, is wholly alien to the Oriental, just as it was wholly alien to the Greek. For the man who lives in a pre-industrial world, time moves at a slow and easy pace; he does not care about each minute, for the good reason that he has not been made conscious of the existence of minutes.

This brings us to a seeming paradox. Acutely aware of the smallest constituent particles of time—of time, as measured by clock-work and train arrivals and the revolutions of machines—industrialized man has to a great extent lost the old awareness of time in its larger divisions. The time of which we have know-ledge is artificial, machine-made time. Of natural, cosmic time, as it is measured out by sun and moon, we are for the most part almost wholly unconscious. Pre-industrial people know time in its daily, monthly and seasonal rhythms. They are aware of sunrise, noon and sunset; of the full moon and the new; of equinox and solstice; of spring and summer, autumn and winter. All the old religions, including Catholic Christianity, have insisted on this daily and seasonal rhythm. Pre-industrial man was never allowed to forget the majestic movements of cosmic time.

Industrialism and urbanism have changed all this. One can live and work in a town without being aware of the daily march of the sun across the sky; without ever seeing the moon and stars. Broadway and Piccadilly are our Milky Way; our con-stellations are outlined in neon tubes. Even changes of season affect the townsman very little. He is the inhabitant of an artificial universe that is, to a great extent, walled off from the world of nature. Outside the walls, time is cosmic and moves with the motion of sun and stars. Within, it is an affair of revolving wheels and is measured in seconds and minutes—at its longest, in eight-hour days and six-day weeks. We have a new consciousness; but it has been purchased at the expense of the old consciousness.

NEW-FASHIONED CHRISTMAS

From *The Olive Tree* (1936)

THE name is still the same; but the thing is almost unrecognizably different from what Charles Dickens meant by 'Christmas'. For example, there was no tree at Dingley Dell, and, except for five shillings to Sam Weller, not a single present was given. Christmas, for Mr Pickwick and his friends, was an affair of copious eating and still more copious drinking, interrupted by bouts of home-made fun and purely domestic horse-play.

For us, three generations later, the word connotes the Prince Consort's imported Teutonic evergreen; connotes all those endless presents, which it is such a burden to buy and such an embarrassment to receive; connotes restaurants, dance halls, theatres, cabarets—all the highly organized, professional entertainments provided by the astute business men who run the amusement industry. Only the name connects the new-fashioned Christmas with the Pickwickian festival.

The tree, of course, was a mere accident. If Queen Victoria had married a Frenchman we should probably be giving one another *étrennes* and ushering in the year with a series of calls on the most remote and the most personally antipathetic of our innumerable relations. (Relations, in France, *are* innumerable.) As it was, she took to herself a prince from the land of tannenbaums. It is therefore to a tannenbaum's green branches, and upon Christmas Day, that we attach our gifts.

The tree, I repeat, was an accident, a thing outside the realm of determinism, a product of personal idiosyncrasy. But all the other changes in our Christmas habits, which have taken place since Dickens wrote Dingley Dell, are the results of great impersonal processes. During Dickens's lifetime, and still more rapidly after his death, industrial production enormously and continuously increased. But production cannot increase unless there is a corresponding increase in consumption. It became necessary to stimulate consumption, to provide the home public with reasons, or, better still, with compelling unreasons, for consuming. Hence the rise of advertisement, and hence the gradual and, as time went on, the more and more deliberate canalization into industrially profitable channels of all such common human impulses and emotions as lent themselves to the process.

The producer who succeeds in thus canalizing some universal human urge opens up for himself and his successors an inexhaustible gold mine. Thus, art and industry have flourished from time immemorial in the rich soil of bereavement and the fear of death. Weddings have been almost as profitable to commerce as funerals, and within the last few years an American man of genius has discovered how even filial affection may be made a justification for increased consumption; the florists and candy manufacturers of the United States have reason to bless the inventor of Mother's Day.

The love of excitement is as deeply planted in human nature as the love of a mother; the desire for change, for novelty, for a relief from the monotony of every day, as strong as sexual desire or the terror of death. Men have instituted festivals and holidays to satisfy these cravings. Mr Pickwick's Christmas was a typical feast day of the old style—a time of jollification and excitement, a gaudily glittering 'captain jewel in the carcanet' of grey, uneventful days. Psychologically, it performed its function. Not economically, however—that is, so far as *we* are concerned. The Pickwickian Christmas did very little to stimulate consumption; it was mainly a gratuitous festivity. A few vintners and distillers and poulterers were the only people whom it greatly profited financially. This was a state of things which an ever-increasingly efficient industrialism could not possibly afford to tolerate. Christmas, accordingly, was canalized. The deep festal impulse of man was harnessed and made to turn a very respectable little wheel in the mills of industry. Today Christmas is an important economic event. The distributors of goods spend large sums in advertising potential gifts, and (since the man who pays the piper calls the tune) the newspapers reinforce their advertisements by fostering a notion that the mutual goodwill of modern Christians can be expressed only by the exchange of manufactured articles.

The last thirty years have witnessed the promotion of inn-keeping and showmanship to the rank of major commercial enterprises. Major commercial enterprises spend money on advertising. Therefore, newspapers are always suggesting that a good time can be enjoyed only by those who take what is offered them by entertainment manufacturers. The Dickensian Christmas-at-Home receives only perfunctory lip-service from a press which draws a steady income from the catering and amusement trades. Home-made fun is gratuitous, and gratuitousness is something which an industrialized world cannot afford to tolerate.

LITERATURE AND EXAMINATIONS

From *The Olive Tree* (1936)

IT happens on the average once every three or four months. The postman drops into my letter-box an envelope addressed in an unfamiliar writing and postmarked anywhere from Oslo to Algiers. Opening it, I find a letter, sometimes in strange English, sometimes in one of the foreign languages with which an ordinarily cultured person is supposed to be familiar. The writer begins by an apology. He (or as often she) is sorry to trouble me, but the fact is that he or she is a student at the university of X or Y or Z, and that, in order to obtain his or her doctorate of Letters, Diploma of Pedagogy, Bachelorship of Modern Languages, Aggregation to the University, or whatever the thing may happen to be called, he or she is writing a thesis about my books—or more often about some particular aspect of my books, such as their style, their construction, the influence upon them of other books, the idea of God in them, their *Weltanschauung* or *Geschlechtsphilosophie*. This being so, will I kindly furnish biographical material, a bibliography of all the reviews and criticisms written in every language, together with copies of such books as the writer happens to have been unable to obtain. In many cases the letter ends with an appeal to my better feelings: will I please do everything that is asked of me, because, if I don't, the writer will be unable to obtain the coveted post at the local University, Lycée, Gymnasium, Preparatoria, or what not, and will have to be content with a job as a teacher in an elementary school.

My feelings when one of these letters arrives are extremely mixed. That I should be treated as though I were a classical author of some earlier century, simultaneously amuses and depresses me, tickles my self-esteem and at the same time punctures it. I like very naturally to think that I am being read; but the idea that I am being *studied* fills me, after the first outburst of laughter, with a deepening gloom. There is something extremely disagreeable about being treated as though one were dead when one supposes—perhaps (and this is the really disquieting thought) mistakenly—that one is still very much alive. Nor is the anticipation of posthumous Fame any compensating satisfaction. For to be sufficiently famous to deserve elaborate study in a modern university is quite humiliatingly easy. Merely to have published is now a sufficient claim to academic attention. As time passes and the numbers of aspirants to diplomas and doctorates continues to pile up, it becomes increasingly difficult to find any significant aspect of a good writer's work which has not already formed the subject of a thesis. The candidate for academic honours has no choice but to study the insignificant aspects of a good writer's work or else the work, not yet explored, because universally deemed not worth exploring, of a bad writer. Universities do me the honour of treating me as though I were defunct and a classic; but it is an honour, alas, that I share with Flecknoe and Pixéricourt, with Hormann von Hofmannswaldau and Nahum Tate.

Walter Raleigh used to say that the teaching of literature always verged on the absurd. He understated the case. The teaching of literature often oversteps the verge and tumbles headlong into the most grotesque absurdity. It is absurd, for example, that students should be forced to spend months and years of their lives on the study of writers who are, by universal consent, of no importance whatsoever. It is equally absurd that they should spend months and years on the study of unimportant aspects of the work of good writers. Very many of the scores of theses produced each year in the various universities of the world are totally pointless. But the teaching of literature produces other absurdities no less monstrous than the learned thesis about a trivial theme. Comparatively few students aspire to specialized learning. For every doctor there are hundreds of bachelors. These obtain their degrees by retailing at second hand a little of the learning and a good deal of the literary criticism of others. Fashions in criticism change, and the candidate must be able to regurgitate the judgment in vogue in academic circles at the time of his ordeal. Success in literary examinations comes to those who know, among other things, what formulae happen, momentarily, to be correct.

What applies to literature applies also to the fine arts. For there are now academic institutions which actually give people degrees in art—minor degrees for those who know a list of dates and can repeat the proper ritual *mantras* about pictures and churches and statues; higher degrees to those who undertake profound original researches into the work of the deservedly neglected artists of the past.

The ultimate cause for this on the whole deplorable state of things is economic. Degrees have a definite cash value. The possession of a given diploma may make all the difference (as my correspondents so often point out in their appeals to my better feelings) between low wages and a low social position in an elementary school and good wages, with considerable social prestige, in the hierarchy of secondary education. Literature and fine arts figure in most curricula at the present time; men and women aspire to teach these subjects; headmasters and education authorities want to be able to distinguish between those who are 'qualified' to teach them and those who are not; universities oblige by creating faculties of literature and fine arts, complete with all the apparatus of diplomas, degrees and doctorates.

Now it is obviously necessary that, for examination purposes, literature and the fine arts should convert themselves, at any rate partially, into parodies of the exact sciences. Literature and art appeal as much to the affective and conative as to the merely cognitive side of man's being. But if you are going to give people marks for literature and art, you must ask them questions that can be answered correctly or incorrectly, you must set them tasks which can be performed only by dint of persevering industriousness. Candidates for the lower degrees will be required, like candidates for the lower degrees in chemistry, say, or biology, to read text-books and do 'practical' work. (In the case of literature, this practical work consists, like the theoretical work, in reading. But whereas theoretical reading is a reading of text-books, practical reading is a reading of the original texts.) Candidates for the higher degrees are expected, like the prospective doctor of science, to do a piece of original research and record their discoveries in a thesis. Even the laboratory methods of exact science are parodied. Literature does not lend itself to being weighed or measured; but at least its material embodiments can be minutely observed and accurately reproduced. The editing of texts has become a branch of microscopy.

It is quite true, of course, that literature and the fine arts have non-literary and non-artistic aspects. They provide important documents in the fields, for example, of social and economic history, of psychology, of philology and the philosophy of language. Moreover, writers and artists employ techniques of expression which profitably lend themselves to scientific analysis. Thus, the *alchimie du verbe*, as Rimbaud called it, can be made to yield some at least of its strange secrets; the geometry and optics of picture-making are worthy of the most serious study. In so far as they are not literature and not art, literature and art can be subjected most fruitfully to the methods of science. And, in effect, much excellent work in history, psychology and so forth has been done by the writers of supposedly literary and artistic theses. All would be well if universities would insist that such work is frankly historical, psychological and the rest, and that it has little or nothing to do with literature as literature, or with art as art. But unfortunately this necessary distinction is not drawn. Under the present dispensation, absurd pseudo-scientific research—into the date, shall we say, of John Chalkhill's second marriage, into the indebtedness of Shadwell to Molière—is as freely encouraged as genuinely scientific research carried out for the purpose of establishing significant relations between one set of facts and another. Moreover, the scientifically treatable, non-literary and non-artistic aspects of literature and art are kept hopelessly mixed up with their purely literary and artistic aspects. Candidates are given marks for displaying symptoms, not merely of knowledge, but also of sensibility and judgment—other people's sensibility, in general practice, and other people's judgment. Perfectly good scientific work has to be accompanied by the repetition of the *mantras* of fashionable criticism. The aesthetic heart must be worn, all through the weary hours of the final examination, palpitating on the sleeve. Every candidate for the bachelorship or doctorate is expected to overflow with the pious phrases of 'appreciation'. The present examination system is calculated to produce the literary and artistic equivalents of Tartuffe and Pecksniff.

That men should hypocritically pay the tribute that philistinism owes to culture is greatly to be desired. The tendency to be realistic and hard-boiled is as dangerous in the sphere of culture as in that of politics. You cannot appeal to the humanitarianism of a fascist who starts out with the realistic assumption that because, in fact, might generally prevails, might is therefore right and should never make any concessions at all. Similarly you cannot appeal to the cultural piety of a low-brow who thinks that, because most human beings are like himself, low-browism is therefore right and ought to triumph over high-browism. Without moral hypocrisy and intellectual snobbery, the decencies of life would lead a most precarious existence.

Intellectual snobbery, I insist, is an excellent thing; but, as of all excellent things, there may be too much of it. An examination system that encourages the candidate for a degree to adorn his non-literary and non-artistic knowledge of literature and art with a veneer of 'appreciative' cant is calculated to produce an excessive number of cultural Pecksniffs, each convinced, on the strength of his diploma, that he is always right. Under a more rational system of education, degrees in literature and art would not be given. Literary and artistic documents would, however, be used as the material of scientific researches in other fields. Feats of mere industry for industry's sake, such as the compilation of theses about writers valueless from a literary point of view and of no particular historical, psychological, economic or other interest, would be discouraged. The application of exact scientific methods to the typography of old books could safely be left to the voluntary enthusiasm of Nature's philatelists and crossword puzzlers. Meanwhile, of course, efforts would be made to encourage students to read and to look at works of art. Groups would be organized for the reading of papers and the discussion of literary and artistic problems. There would also be exercises in the art of writing clearly and correctly. In this way the natural sensibilities of the students might be developed, and the tendency, so much encouraged by the examination system, to mug up other people's judgments and repeat them, mechanically and without reflection, severely discouraged. At the same time students would be able to feel that their scientific work—the study of the significant non-literary and non-artistic aspects of literary and artistic documents—was genuinely valuable and enlightening, not the mere parody of scientific work that, too often, they are expected to do at present.

As things stand at present, it would be very difficult to make the kind of changes I have indicated above, for the simple reason that there are very many people who, for economic reasons, *want* degrees in literature and the fine arts. The employers of academic labour regard such degrees as qualifications for comparatively well-paid posts. It will be impossible to change the existing examination system until they have been educated to think differently.

SCIENCE, LIBERTY AND PEACE

(1947) (an extract)

'SCIENCE' is an abstract word, and when we are trying to think about concrete political and economic problems, it is best to talk concretely, not of science but of the people who work in the various scientific fields, from the fields of uncontaminated theory and disinterested research into basic problems to those of applied science and technology. Assuming that the abolition of war is desirable, we proceed to ask ourselves how scientific workers can help to achieve this end.

1. As individuals or in organized groups, scientific workers can take three kinds of action against war. There is, first, the possibility of negative action in the form of a refusal, on conscientious grounds, to participate in work having as its purpose the killing, torture or enslavement of human beings. Christianity once insisted, and Buddhism still insists, upon the importance of 'right livelihood'. There are certain professions so intrinsically harmful that no individual ought to practise them. In the eyes of medieval Catholic theologians, for example, the profession of a moneylender or of a speculator was beyond the pale: they held that man could not live by usury and the manipulation of the commodity markets, and still be regarded as a Christian. Similarly, for Buddha and his followers, a man could not be regarded as a Buddhist, if he made his living by the manufacture of arms or intoxicants. Men of science and technologists would do well, as individuals and in their national and international organizations, to consider the problem of right livelihood in its relation to their own contemporary activities. Is it possible to work on the development of instruments of ever more indiscriminate slaughter and to remain—not a good Christian or a good Buddhist; for in scientific and technological circles religion is now out of fashion—but a good human being? Is it possible to go on believing that one is working for the good of mankind,

while applying the results of disinterested research in ways which demonstrably increase the power of the ruling capitalist or governmental minority at the expense of personal liberty and local and professional self-government? These and similar questions need to be asked and carefully answered by scientific workers—asked and answered, if possible, on the level of their international organizations. Meanwhile it is to be hoped and perhaps expected that a certain number of individual scientists and technicians will take the negative stand against war and the centralization of power which is war's inevitable accompaniment, by refusing to collaborate in any project whose purpose is the destruction or enslavement of human beings.

2. Negative action is good so far as it goes, but it needs to be supplemented by action of a positive and constructive kind. Such positive action may be classified under two heads: (a) action which takes its start in politics, to end in the field of science: and (b) action which takes its start in science, to end in politics.

(a) Several suggestions have recently been made for the political control, in the interests of humanity, of the activities of scientists and technologists. Thus, in the course of an interesting two-day debate in the House of Lords (May 29 and 30, 1945) Lord Vansittart urged the necessity of subjecting all German laboratories, whether attached to universities or supported by the state or by private industrialists, to strict supervision over a long term of years. Only in this way, he claimed, could the danger of a war of revenge, waged with new 'secret weapons', be avoided. More realistically, Lord Brabazon proposed that this supervision of scientific developments should not be confined exclusively to the defeated nations—nations whose opportunities for the large-scale manufacture of new weapons would, for many years at least, be small. His suggestion was that, under the final peace treaties, an international committee of inspection should be constituted, having authority to enter laboratories and factories in any part of the world. In Lord Brabazon's view, the only alternative to such a scheme of international inspection would be an armament race between Britain and the United States on the one hand and the rest of the world on the other. By intensive research the Anglo-Saxon group might hope to obtain the lead in such a race, and so discourage attack by other powers. Lord Brabazon's speech was made before the dropping of the first atomic bomb. As things now stand, the United States and Britain already possess an enormous lead in the post-war armament race. For a few years they may keep that lead. Then other nations (unless, of course, they are previously blown to bits by the present possessors of the bomb, or unless reason, surrender of absolute sovereignty and world government come to replace nationalism) will be supplied by their scientists with the same or even better methods for manufacturing atomic missiles. Meanwhile the desirability of an international inspectorate charged with preserving humanity from the triumphs of science is even greater now than it was before Hiroshima. The existence of an international inspectorate would involve the adoption of another security measure, advocated in the course of the same debate by Lord Strabolgi—namely, the pooling of all scientific discoveries considered by competent experts to be actually or potentially a danger to mankind.

Similar suggestions have been made on the other side of the Atlantic, and it now remains to be seen whether, and to what extent, the United Nations will act upon them. Meanwhile Messrs Truman, Attlee and King have decided to keep such secrets as their scientists and engineers still possess until 'enforceable safeguards' against their use for destructive purposes can be devised.

What is to be the nature of those 'enforceable safeguards'? As yet, it would seem, nobody has any very clear idea. In principle, the proposals for a pooling of dangerous knowledge and for an international inspectorate are excellent; and, to some, the theory of an 'international police force' seems attractive and even workable. But, alas, from principle to application and from theory to practice the road is long and hard. Two disturbing questions inevitably propound themselves. First, will the various national governments concerned agree to act upon these suggestions? Second, if they do agree, will they and the men of science they employ consent to play the game according to the internationally imposed rules? In attempting to answer these questions one must weigh the power of enlightened self-interest against the power of nationalistic passions and prejudices. Enlightened self-interest will unquestioningly vote for world government, international inspection and the pooling of information. But unfortunately, in some of the most important issues of life, human beings do not act from considerations of enlightened self-interest. If they did, we should now be living in something very like paradise. In the field of international politics, as we have seen, the gravest decisions are always taken, not by reasonable adults but by boy-gangsters. Despite the lessons of Hiroshima and Nagasaki, it is quite possible that some national governments will refuse to allow their laboratories and factories to be inspected—and, of course, the refusal of even one government will entail the general abandonment of the scheme. Alternatively, the principle of international inspection will be accepted; but at first some and then (when suspicion has been aroused) all the governments concerned will conspire with the scientists in their employ to carry on research in caves or forests or mountain fastnesses, where no prying eye can see what they are up to. It may perhaps seem unlikely that workers trained in the methods of science should support their political bosses in machinations so manifestly senseless, as well as immoral. But it is not because men have learned to behave rationally in the laboratory that they can be trusted to behave rationally toward foreigners and unpopular minorities, or even toward their own wives and children. Until a very few years ago the best scientific and technological education available was given in Germany; but most of the persons who received that education not only worked for the Nazi bosses, but believed in their doctrines and were swayed by the nationalistic passions which they so skilfully exploited. The case of Germany is not unique. In all countries nationalistic passions (of the same kind as were manifested in Germany, but at a somewhat lower level of intensity) are almost as common among scientists and technicians as in other classes of society. In spite of their training (perhaps, indeed, owing to the narrowly specialized character of that training, because of it), scientists and technicians are perfectly capable of the most dangerously irrational prejudice, nor are they immune to deceitful propaganda. The same men who reject as superstitious the belief in a transcendent and immanent spiritual Reality beyond and within phenomena, prove by their actions that they find no difficulty in worshipping as a supreme god whichever one of the world's fifty-odd nations they happen to belong to, and in accepting the infallibility of the local Foreign Office and the quasi-divinity of the local political boss. In view of all this we need not be surprised if the plans for an international inspectorate and the pooling of scientific knowledge should fail in practice to produce the good results expected of them.

(b) We must now consider the specifically scientific action which might be taken by men of science and technicians with a view to diminishing the probability of war and so to increasing the sum of human liberty. Such action can only be taken on the plane of applied science. Basic research is essentially disinterested. Men undertake it because, in the words used by the boy Clerk Maxwell, they want to find out 'what's the go' of things—to discover how nature works and how its parts are related within a causal system. What is subsequently done with the results of disinterested research is something which the researcher cannot foresee, and for which he is not responsible. Thus, Clerk Maxwell's own adult curiosity to find out the go of such things as light and magnetism led him to certain conclusions, and these conclusions have since been utilized by technicians for the development of instruments which are now used, in the main, for the dissemination of maudlin drama, cigarette advertising, bad music and government-sponsored or capitalist-sponsored propaganda. Clerk Maxwell would probably have been horrified by all these uses of the radio, and he is, of course, in no way to blame for them. In practice, it would seem, basic research cannot be planned, except perhaps to the extent of subsidizing inquiry into branches of knowledge, which for whatever reason, appear to have been unduly neglected. If the facilities for research are supplied, men and women with an overpowering desire to find out the go of things will always be forthcoming to make use of them. The planning of scientific activity with a view to achieving certain predetermined political, social and economic ends must begin at the point where the results of disinterested research are applied to the solution of practical problems. Individually and through their professional organizations, scientists and technicians could do a great deal to direct the planning toward humane and reasonable ends.

In theory everyone agreed that applied science was made for man and not man for applied science. In practice great masses of human beings have again and again been sacrificed to applied science. The conflict between science, as it has been applied up to the present, and human interests was clearly stated by Thorstein Veblen in his *Science in the Modern World*. In this essay Veblen distinguishes between what he calls the pragmatic and the scientific point of view. Pragmatically human beings know pretty well what is good for them, and have developed myths and fairy tales, proverbs and popular philosophies, behaviour-patterns and moralities, in order to illustrate and embody their findings about life. The findings of science—especially of science as applied for the benefit of the holders of centralized economic and political power—are frequently in conflict with humanity's pragmatic values, and this conflict has been and still is the source of much unhappiness, frustration and bitterness. The enormous practical importance of the clash between scientific (or rather applied-scientific) values and pragmatic human values is stressed in an editorial which appeared in a recent issue (July 22, 1945) of the leading British scientific journal *Nature*. In maintaining industrial morals 'the central difficulty', writes the author of this article, 'is essentially the inevitable opposition which develops between the scientific approach to the human problems of production and the political approach of the administrator, trained in the method of accommodation and compromise. The balancing of opinion and the compromise of different points of view, which is the essence of the political process, may be totally at odds with the scientific approach to questions of industrial management. What is required is not the surrender of scientific principles of established accuracy, or the ignoring of accepted fact, but the combination or integration of both the political and scientific approach in a solution which satisfies both the scientific and the psychological or political requirements.'

Let us begin by noting that in any discussion of economic or political problems, the word 'integration' is always a danger signal; for it is always tacitly assumed that the work of integration is carried out by somebody standing above the processes and persons to be integrated. In other words, whenever people call for 'integration' they are always calling for the exercise of centralized governmental power and for yet another extension of the process of institutionalization. But power is always corrupting, and no human being or group of human beings is to be trusted with too much of it for too long. When science is applied in such a way as to create a form of production, which cannot be run efficiently without coming into sharp conflict with fundamental human values, and which therefore continually calls for the intervention of a governmental authority having power to 'integrate' the conflicting persons and points of view, it may be fairly presumed that the application of the results of disinterested research has been, humanly speaking, misguided and undesirable. Up to the present time applied science has not been used mainly or primarily for the benefit of humanity at large, or (to put the matter less abstractly) for the benefit of individual men and women, considered as personalities each one of which is capable, given suitable material and social conditions, of a moral and spiritual development amounting, in some cases, to a total transfiguration; rather man has been used for applied science, for the technicians who enjoy designing more and more complicated gadgets, and for the financial and governmental interests which profit by the centralization of power. If applied science is henceforward to be used for man, technicians and scientists will have to adopt a professional policy, consciously and deliberately designed to serve fundamental human needs and to forward the causes of peace and personal liberty. Such a policy could not be worked out in detail except by an international organization of scientific workers, highly trained in their respective fields, so that each could contribute his or her share of skill or information toward the realization of the common end—namely, the welfare, liberty and peace of the individuals composing the human race. It would be absurd for me to try to anticipate the findings of this hypothetical group of experts; but it is possible, without too much presumption, to indicate in a general way a few of the lines which their discussion would have to follow.

Humanity's primary requirement is a sufficiency of food; but it is primarily by considerations of power that the policies of national governments are at present dictated. The ruling minorities of the world invariably contrive to have enough, and (to judge by the disgusting descriptions of recent diplomatic banquets) more than enough to eat; consequently they tend to take food for granted and to think first, and at times almost exclusively, in terms of the questions: Who shall bully whom? But the great majority of the men, women and children on this planet are in no position to take food for granted. Their first and often their exclusive concern is the next meal. The question as to who shall bully whom is of hardly more than academic interest to them. They would like, of course, to be left in peace to go their own way; but they know by bitter experience that, under the present dispensation, there will always be a ruling minority to order them about, to bully and badger them in the name of the divine Nation, the omniscient Party, the sacred Principles of this or that political doctrine. They are therefore unable to take much interest in the national and international policies, which are the prime concern of the well-fed power lovers at the top of the social pyramid.

At the San Francisco Conference the only problems discussed were problems of power. The basic problem of mankind—the problem of getting enough to eat—was relegated to an obscure international committee on agriculture. And yet it is surely obvious that if genuine international agreement is ever to be reached and preserved, it must be an agreement with regard to problems which, first, are of vital interest to the great masses of humanity and which, second, are capable of solution without resort to war or the threat of war. The problems of power are primarily the concern of the ruling few, and the nature of power is essentially expansive, so that there is not the least prospect of power problems being solved, when one expanding system collides with another expanding system, except by means of organized, scientific violence or war. But war on the modern scale shatters the thin, precarious crust of civilization and precipitates vast numbers of human beings into an abyss of misery and slow death, of moral apathy or positive and frenzied diabolism. If politicians were sincere in their loudly expressed desire for peace, they would do all they could to by-pass the absolutely insoluble problems of power by concentrating all their attention, during international conferences and diplomatic discussion, on the one great problem which every member of the human race is concerned to solve—the one great problem which not only does not require military violence for its solution, but which, for the world at large, is wholly insoluble so long as the old games of militarism and power politics continue to be played. The first item on the agenda of every meeting between the representatives of the various nations should be: *How are all men, women and children to get enough to eat?*

It is fashionable nowadays to say that Malthus was wrong, because he did not foresee that improved methods of transportation can now guarantee that food surpluses produced in one area shall be quickly and cheaply transferred to another, where there is a shortage. But first of all, modern transportation methods break down whenever the power politicians resort to modern war, and even when the fighting stops they are apt to remain disrupted long enough to guarantee the starvation of millions of persons. And, secondly, no country in which population has outstripped the local food supply can, under present conditions, establish a claim on the surpluses of other countries without paying for them in cash or exports. Great Britain and the other countries in western Europe, which cannot feed their dense populations, have been able, in times of peace, to pay for the food they imported by means of the export of manufactured goods. But industrially backward India and China—countries in which Malthus' nightmare has come true with a vengeance and on the largest scale—produce few manufactured goods, consequently lack the means to buy from underpopulated areas the food they need. But when and if they develop mass-producing industries to the point at which they are able to export enough to pay for the food their rapidly expanding populations require, what will be the effect upon world trade and international politics? Japan had to export manufactured goods in order to pay for the food that could not be produced on the overcrowded home islands. Goods produced by workers with a low standard of living came into competition with goods produced by the better paid workers of the West, and undersold them. The West's retort was political and consisted of the imposing of high tariffs, quotas and embargoes. To these restrictions on her trade Japan's answer was the plan for creating a vast Asiatic empire at the expense of China and of the Western imperialist powers. The result was war. What will happen when India and China are as highly industrialized as pre-war Japan and seek to exchange their low-priced manufactured goods for food, in competition with Western powers, whose standard of living is a great deal higher than theirs? Nobody can foretell the future; but undoubtedly the rapid industrialization of Asia (with equipment, let it be remembered, of the very latest and best post-war design) is pregnant with the most dangerous possibilities.

It is at this point that internationally organized scientists and technicians might contribute greatly to the cause of peace by planning a world-wide campaign, not merely for greater food production, but also (and this is the really important point) for regional self-sufficiency in food production. Greater food production can be obtained relatively easily by the opening of the earth's vast subarctic regions at present completely sterile. Spectacular progress has recently been made in this direction by the agricultural scientists of the Soviet Union; and presumably what can be done in Siberia can also be done in northern Canada. Powerful ice-breakers are already being used to solve the problems of transportation by sea and river; and perhaps commercial submarines, specially equipped for travelling under the ice, may in the future ensure a regular service between Arctic ports and the rest of the world. Any increase of the world's too scanty food supply is to be welcomed. But our rejoicings must be tempered by two considerations. First, the surpluses of food produced by the still hypothetical Arctic granaries of Siberia and Canada will have to be transferred by ship, plane and rail to the overpopulated areas of the world. This means that no supplies would be available in war-time. Second, possession of food-producing Arctic areas constitutes a natural monopoly, and this natural monopoly will not, as in the past, be in the hands of politically weak nations, such as Argentina and Australia, but will be controlled by the two great power systems of the post-war period—the Russian power system and the Anglo-American power system. That their monopolies of food surpluses will be used as weapons in the game of power politics seems more than probable. 'Lead us not into temptation.' The opening up of the Arctic will be undoubtedly a great good. But it will also be a great temptation for the power politicians—a temptation to exploit a natural monopoly in order to gain influence and finally control over hitherto independent countries, in which population has outstripped the food supply.

It would seem, then, that any scientific and technological campaign aimed at the fostering of international peace and political and personal liberty must, if it is to succeed, increase the total planetary food supply by increasing the various regional supplies to the point of self-sufficiency. Recent history makes it abundantly clear that nations, as at present constituted, are quite unfit to have extensive commercial dealings with one another. International trade has always, hitherto, gone hand in hand with war, imperialism and the ruthless exploitation of industrially backward peoples by the highly industrialized powers. Hence the desirability of reducing international trade to a minimum, until such time as nationalist passions lose their intensity and it becomes possible to establish some form of world government. As a first step in this direction, scientific and technical means must be found for making it possible for even the most densely populated countries to feed their inhabitants. The improvement of existing food plants and domestic animals; the acclimatization in hitherto inhospitable regions of plants that have proved useful elsewhere; the reduction of the present enormous waste of food by the improvement of insect controls and the multiplication of refrigerating units; the more systematic exploitation of seas and lakes as sources of food; the development of entirely new foods, such as edible yeasts; the synthesizing of sugars as a food for such edible yeasts; the synthezising of chlorophyll so as to make direct use of solar energy in food production—these are a few of the lines along which important advances might be made in a relatively short time.

Hardly less important than regional self-sufficiency in food is self-sufficiency in power for industry, agriculture and transportation. One of the contributing causes of recent wars has been international competition for the world's strictly localized sources of petroleum, and the current jockeying for position in the Middle East, where all the surviving great powers have staked out claims to Persian, Mesopotamian and Arabian oil, bodes ill for the future. Organized science could diminish these temptations to armed conflict by finding means for providing all countries, whatever their natural resources, with a sufficiency of power. Water power has already been pretty well exploited. Besides, over large areas of the earth's surface there are no mountains and therefore no sources of hydro-electric power. But across the plains where water stands almost still, the air often moves in strong and regular currents. Small windmills have been turning for centuries; but the use of large-scale wind turbines is still, strangely enough, only in the experimental stage. Until recently the direct use of solar power has been impracticable, owing to the technical difficulty of constructing suitable reflectors. A few months ago, however, it was announced that Russian engineers had developed a cheap and simple method for constructing paraboloid mirrors of large size, capable of producing superheated steam and even of melting iron. This discovery could be made to contribute very greatly to the decentralization of production and population and the creation of a new type of agrarian society making use of cheap and inexhaustible power for the benefit of individual small-holders or self-governing, co-operative groups. For the peoples of such tropical countries as India and Africa the new device for directly harnessing solar power should be of enormous and enduring benefit —unless, of course, those at present possessing economic and political power should choose to build mass-producing factories around enormous mirrors, thus perverting the invention to their own centralistic purposes, instead of encouraging its small-scale use for the benefit of individuals and village communities. The technicians of solar power will be confronted with a clear-cut choice. They can work either for the completer enslavement of the industrially backward peoples of the tropics, or for their progressive liberation from the twin curses of poverty and servitude to political and economic bosses.

The storage of the potentialities of power is almost as important as the production of power. One of the most urgent tasks before applied science is the development of some portable source of power to replace petroleum—a most undesirable fuel from the political point of view, since deposits of it are rare and unevenly distributed over the earth's surface, thus constituting natural monopolies which, when in the hands of strong nations, are used to increase their strength at the expense of their neighbours and, when possessed by weak ones, are coveted by the strong and constitute almost irresistible temptation to imperialism and war. From the political and human point of view, the most desirable substitute for petroleum would be an efficient battery for storing the electric power produced by water, wind or sun. Further research into atomic structure may perhaps suggest new methods for the construction of such a battery.

Meanwhile it is possible that means may be devised, within the next few years, for applying atomic energy to the purposes of peace, as it is now being applied to those of war. Would not this technological development solve the whole problem of power for industry and transportation? The answer to this question may turn out to be simultaneously affirmative and negative. The problems of power may indeed be solved—but solved in the wrong way, by which I mean in a way favourable to centralization and the ruling minority, not for the benefit of individuals and co-operative, self-governing groups. If the raw material of atomic energy must be sought in radio-active deposits, occurring sporadically, here and there, over the earth's surface, then we have natural monopoly with all its undesirable political consequences, all its temptations to power politics, war, imperialistic aggression and exploitation. But of course it is always possible that other methods of releasing atomic energy may be discovered—methods that will not involve the use of uranium. In this case there will be no natural monopoly. But the process of releasing atomic energy will always be a very difficult and complicated affair, to be accomplished only on the largest scale and in the most elaborately equipped factories. Furthermore, whatever political agreements may be made, the fact that atomic energy possesses unique destructive potentialities will always constitute a temptation to the boy-gangster who lurks within every patriotic nationalist. And even if a world government should be set up within a fairly short space of time, this will not necessarily guarantee peace. The Pax Romana was a very uneasy affair, troubled at almost every imperial death by civil strife over the question of succession. So long as the lust for power persists as a human trait—and in persons of a certain kind of physique and temperament this lust is overmasteringly strong —no political arrangement, however well contrived, can guarantee peace. For such men the instruments of violence are as fearfully tempting as are, to others, the bodies of women. Of all instruments of violence, those powered by atomic energy are the most decisively destructive; and for power lovers, even under a system of world government, the temptation to resort to these all too simple and effective means for gratifying their lust will be great indeed. In view of all this, we must conclude that atomic energy is, and for a long time is likely to remain, a source of industrial power that is, politically and humanly speaking, in the highest degree undesirable.

It is not necessary in this place, nor am I competent, to enter any further into the hypothetical policy of internationally organized science. If that policy is to make a real contribution toward the maintenance of peace and the spread of political and personal liberty, it must be patterned throughout along the decentralist lines laid down in the preceding discussion of the two basic problems of food and power. Will scientists and technicians collaborate to formulate and pursue some such policy as that which has been adumbrated here? Or will they permit themselves, as they have done only too often in the past, to become the conscious or unconscious instruments of militarists, imperialists and a ruling oligarchy of capitalistic or governmental bosses? Time alone will show. Meanwhile, it is to be hoped that all concerned will carefully consider a suggestion made by Dr Gene Weltfish in the September, 1945, issue of the *Scientific Monthly*. Before embarking upon practice, all physicians swear a professional oath—the oath of Hippocrates—that they will not take improper advantage of their position, but always remember their responsibilities toward suffering humanity. Technicians and scientists, proposes Dr Weltfish, should take a similar oath in some such words as the following: 'I pledge myself that I will use my knowledge for the good of humanity and against the destructive forces of the world and the ruthless intent of men; and that I will work together with my fellow scientists of whatever nation, creed or colour for these our common ends.'

VARIATIONS ON EL GRECO

From *Themes and Variations* (1950)

IN 1541, when Domenikos Theotokopoulos was born, his native island of Crete had been for more than three centuries under Venetian rule. Trade had followed the imperial flag, but not culture. In language, in thought, in art, the island remained as what it had been ever since the People of the Sea finally broke the Minoan power—a part of Greece. In the Cretan schools young men studied the philosophers of ancient Athens and the theologians of Christian Byzantium, Byzantine paintings and Byzantine mosaics adorned the churches, and even in the revolutionary sixteenth century the Cretan artists went their traditional way without paying the smallest attention to what had been happening in near-by Italy. Their pictures were two-dimensional, non-realistic, innocent of perspective and chiaroscuro. So far as they were concerned, Giotto and Masaccio, to say nothing of Raphael and Michelangelo and Titian, might never have existed.

Young Domenikos received a sound Greek education and studied painting under the best masters of the island. Not, however, for very long. In Candia one could see along with the other importations from the mainland, examples of Venetian painting. The orthodox might shake their heads. What a way to treat the Mother of God! And that indecently human personage—was that supposed to be the Pantocrator? But to a young man of original and enquiring mind their very unorthodoxy must have seemed attractive. They were tokens from a world where the artist was his own master, where too he might make technical experiments, where he was free to see and represent all the things which, for the Byzantines, simply didn't exist. Moreover, this world of artistic liberty was also a world where a man could make his fortune. Venice was rich; Crete, miserably poor. There was no future for a man in Candia; but on the mainland, on the mainland . . .

In the early fifteen-sixties, when the young immigrant from Crete first stepped ashore, Venice was at the height of her artistic glory. Titian was a very old man, but painting as well as, or indeed better than, he had ever done in his youth. Tintoretto, his junior by forty years, was hard at work, transforming the principles of High Renaissance composition into those of the Baroque. Still in his youthful prime, Veronese was effortlessly turning out enormous masterpieces of decorative art. 'Bliss was it in that dawn to be alive.' But, all dawns—the artistic no less than the political, the religious, the sexual—give place to mornings, afternoons and nights. After having worked for several years as 'a disciple of Titian' (to use the phrase by which he was later to be described) Domenikos came to be profoundly dissatisfied with Venetian art. It could hardly have been otherwise. By nature introspective, by nurture a Christian Neo-Platonist and a student of Byzantine art, the young man might admire Venetian technique, but could never approve the uses to which that technique was put. For his taste Venetian art was too pagan, too voluptuous, too decorative, too much concerned with appearances, insufficiently inward and serious. In search of an art more conformable to his own nature and ideals Domenikos migrated in 1570 to Rome. But Rome, alas, proved to be no less disappointing than Venice. The great masters of the High Renaissance were all dead, and their successors were second-rate mannerists, incapable of creating anything new and living parasitically upon the achievements of the past. For Domenikos, the living were without interest and even the mighty dead were not the masters he had been looking for. Of Michelangelo, for example, he complained that the man did not know how to paint —which is a rather violent way of expressing the unquestionable truth that Michelangelo was primarily a sculptor and that his paintings are in some sort translations of sculpture into a language which was not the artist's native tongue. To a young man whose vocation was to express himself, not in marble, not in transcriptions of sculpture, but in colour and the rich texture of oil pigments, the frescoes of the Sistine Chapel were not very instructive.

The artist's stay in Rome lasted for several years. Then, at some date prior to 1577, he undertook yet another migration, this time to Spain. Why to Spain? As usual, we do not know. And when, some years later, during a lawsuit, the same question was put to El Greco himself, he declined to answer. Evidently he was of the opinion that people should mind their own business.

The Cretan's wanderings were now at an end. He settled in Toledo, and there with his wife, Jeronima de las Cuevas, and his son, Jorge Manuel, he remained until his death in 1614. Of his life in Spain, we know only a very little more than we know of his life in Crete and Italy—that is to say, next to nothing. Here are some of the scanty odds and ends of information that have come down to us.

Professionally, El Greco was successful. Many commissions came his way and he was well paid for his work. On several occasions he went to law with his ecclesiastical patrons in order to get his price. He had the reputation of spending his money with a lordly extravagance, and it was said that he paid an orchestra to make music while he ate his meals His apartment on the verge of the great canyon of the Tagus contained twenty-four rooms, most of which, however, were left almost completely unfurnished. Of his own genius he had no doubts. He knew that he painted superlatively well and he was quite ready to say so in public. Moreover, when Philip II and certain of the clergy objected to his pictures on the ground that they did not respect the norms of ecclesiastical art, he steadfastly refused to compromise and went on painting exactly as he thought fit. Like Tintoretto, he modelled small clay figures, with the aid of which he studied effects of lighting and foreshortening. Pacheco, the father-in-law of Velasquez, saw a whole cupboardful of these figures when he visited El Greco shortly before the latter's death. Needless to say, they have all disappeared and along with them has gone the treatise which El Greco wrote on painting. Among the painter's friends were poets, men of learning, eminent ecclesiastics. His library, as we know from the inventory which was made after his death, contained, among other Greek works, the famous *Mystical Theology* of Dionysius the Areo-pagite, together with more recent Italian books on Neo-Platonic philosophy. In the light of this fact, a curious anecdote recorded by Giulio Clovio, one of El Greco's Roman friends, takes on a special significance. 'Yesterday', wrote Clovio in a letter which is still extant, 'I called at his (El Greco's) lodgings to take him for a walk through the city. The weather was very fine. . . . But on entering the studio I was amazed to find the curtains so closely drawn that it was hardly possible to see anything. The painter was sitting in a chair, neither working nor sleeping, and declined to go out with me on the ground that the light of day disturbed his inward light.' From this it would appear that El Greco took more than a theoretical interest in the mystical states described by Dionysius and the Neo-Platonists; he also practised some form of meditation.

Of El Greco's personal appearance we know nothing for certain. The so-called 'self-portrait' may perhaps represent the painter's features; or, on the other hand, it may not. The evidence is inconclusive. At every turn the man eludes us. Only his work remains.

A representational picture is one that 'tells a story'—the story, for example, of the Nativity, the story of Mars and Venus, the story of a certain landscape or a certain person as they appeared at a certain moment of time. But this story is never the whole story. A picture always expresses more than is implicit in its subject. Every painter who tells a story tells it in his own manner, and that manner tells another story superimposed, as it were, upon the first—a story about the painter himself, a story about the way in which one highly gifted individual reacted to his experience of our universe. The first story is told deliberately; the second tells itself independently of the artist's conscious will. He cannot help telling it; for it is the expression of his own intimate being—of the temperament with which he was born, the character which he himself has forged and the unconscious tendencies formed by the interaction of temperament, character and outward circumstances.

Like most of his predecessors and contemporaries, El Greco was mainly a religious painter, a teller of old familiar stories, from the Gospels and the legends of the saints. But he told it in his own peculiar manner, and that manner tells another story so enigmatic that we pore over it in fascinated bewilderment, trying to construe its meaning.

In looking at any of the great compositions of El Greco's maturity, we must always remember that the intention of the artist was neither to imitate nature nor to tell a story with dramatic verisimilitude. Like the Post-Impressionists three centuries later, El Greco used natural objects as the raw material out of which, by a process of calculated distortion, he might create his own world of pictorial forms in pictorial space under pictorial illumination. Within this private universe he situated his religious subject-matter, using it as a vehicle for expressing what he wanted to say about life.

And what *did* El Greco want to say? The answer can only be inferred; but to me, at least, it seems sufficiently clear. Those faces with their uniformly rapturous expression, those hands clasped in devotion or lifted towards heaven, those figures stretched out to the point where the whole inordinately elongated anatomy becomes a living symbol of upward aspiration—all those bear witness to the artist's constant preoccupation with the ideas of mystical religion. His aim is to assert the soul's capacity to come, through effort and through grace, to ecstatic union with the divine Spirit. This idea of union is more and more emphatically stressed as the painter advances in years. The frontier between earth and heaven, which is clearly defined in such works as *The Burial of Count Orgaz* and *The Dream of Philip II*, grows fainter and finally disappears. In the latest version of Christ's Baptism there is no separation of any kind. The forms and colours flow continuously from the bottom of the picture to the top. The two realms are totally fused.

Does this mean that El Greco actually found a perfect pictorial expression for what his contemporary, St Teresa of Avila, called 'the spiritual marriage'? I think not. For all their extraordinary

beauty, these great paintings are strangely oppressive and disquieting. Consciously El Greco was telling two stories—a story
from the Gospels or the legends of the saints, and a story about
mystical union with the divine. But, unconsciously, he told yet
another story, having little or nothing to do with the two he
knew he was telling. All that is disquieting in El Greco pertains
to this third story and is conveyed to the spectator by his highly
individual manner of treating space and the forms by which that
space is occupied.

In the Byzantine art, with which El Greco was familiar in
his youth, there is no third dimension. The figures in the icons
and mosaics are the inhabitants of a Flatland in which there is
no question of perspective. And precisely because there is no
perspective, these figures seem to exist in a celestial universe
having implications of indefinite extension. From ancient and
conservative Byzantium El Greco travelled through time as well
as space to modern Venice. Here, in Titian's paintings, he found
the realistic representation of a third dimension travelling back
from the picture-plane to far-away landscapes of blue mountains
under majestic clouds. And in Tintoretto's compositions he
could study those rocketing centrifugal movements that carry
the spectator's mind beyond the picture-frame and suggest the
endless succession of things and spaces existing in the world
outside.

The nature of El Greco's personality was such that he chose
to combine Byzantium and Venice in the strangest possible way.
His pictures are neither flat nor fully three-dimensional. There
is depth in his private universe, but only a very little of it. From
the picture-plane to the remotest object in the background there
is, in most cases, an apparent distance of only a few feet. On
earth, as in heaven, there is hardly room to swing a cat. Moreover, unlike Tintoretto and the baroque artists of the seventeenth
century, El Greco never hints at the boundlessness beyond the
picture-frame. His compositions are centripetal, turned inwards
on themselves. He is the painter of movement in a narrow room,
of agitation in prison. This effect of confinement is enhanced by

the almost complete absence from his paintings of a landscape background. The whole picture-space is tightly packed with figures, human and divine; and where any chink is left between body and body, we are shown only a confining wall of cloud as opaque as earth, or of earth as fluidly plastic as the clouds. So far as El Greco is concerned, the world of non-human nature is practically non-existent.

No less disquieting than the narrowness of El Greco's universe is the quality of the forms with which he filled it. Everything here is organic, but organic on a low level, organic to a point well below the limit of life's perfection. That is why there is no sensuality in these paintings, nothing of the voluptuous. In a work of art we are charmed and attracted by forms which represent or at least suggest the forms of such objects as we find attractive in nature—flowers, for example, fruits, animals, human bodies in their youthful stength and beauty. In life we are not at all attracted by protoplasm in the raw or by individual organs separated from the organism as a whole. But it is with forms suggestive precisely of such objects that El Greco fills his pictures. Under his brush the human body, when it is naked, loses its bony framework and even its musculature, and becomes a thing of ectoplasm—beautifully appropriate in its strange pictorial context, but not a little uncanny when thought of in the context of real life. And when El Greco clothes his boneless creatures, their draperies become pure abstractions, having the form of something indeterminately physiological.

And here a brief parenthesis is in order. A painter or a sculptor can be simultaneously representational and non-representational. In their architectural backgrounds and, above all, in their draperies, many works, even of the Renaissance and the Baroque, incorporate passages of almost unadulterated abstraction. These are often expressive in the highest degree. Indeed, the whole tone of a representational work may be established, and its inner meaning expressed, by those parts of it which are most nearly abstract. Thus, the pictures of Piero della Francesca leave upon us an impression of calm, of power, of intellectual objectivity and stoical detachment. From those of Cosimo Tura there emanates a sense of disquiet, even of anguish. When we analyse the purely pictorial reasons for our perception of a profound difference in the temperaments of the two artists, we find that a very important part is played by the least representational elements in their pictures—the draperies. In Piero's draperies there are large unbroken surfaces, and the folds are designed to emphasize the elementary solid-geometrical structure of the figures. In Tura's draperies the surfaces are broken up, and there is a profusion of sharp angles, of jagged and flame-like forms. Something analogous may be found in the work of two great painters of a later period, Poussin and Watteau. Watteau's draperies are broken into innumerable tiny folds and wrinkles, so that the colour of a mantle or a doublet is never the same for half an inch together. The impression left upon the spectator is one of extreme sensibility and the most delicate refinement. Poussin's much broader treatment of these almost non-representational accessories seems to express a more masculine temperament and a philosophy of life akin to Piero's noble stoicism.

In some works the non-representational passages are actually more important than the representational. Thus in many of Bernini's statues, only the hands, feet and face are fully representational; all the rest is drapery—that is to say, a writhing and undulant abstraction. It is the same with El Greco's paintings. In some of them a third, a half, even as much as two-thirds of the entire surface is occupied by low-level organic abstractions, to which, because of their representational context, we give the name of draperies, or clouds, or rocks. These abstractions are powerfully expressive and it is through them that, to a considerable extent, El Greco tells the private story that underlies the official subject-matter of his paintings.

At this point the pure abstractionist will come forward with a question. Seeing that the non-representational passages in representational works are so expressive, why should anyone bother with representation? Why trouble to tell a high-level story about recognizable objects when the more important low-level story about the artist's temperament and reactions to life can be told in terms of pure abstractions? I myself have no objection to pure abstractions which, in the hands of a gifted artist, can achieve their own kind of aesthetic perfection. But this perfection, it seems to me, is a perfection within rather narrow limits. The Greeks called the circle 'a perfect figure'. And so it is—one cannot improve on it. And yet a composition consisting of a red circle inscribed within a black square would strike us, for all its perfection, as being a little dull. Even aesthetically the perfect figure of a circle is less interesting than the perfect figure of a young woman. This does not mean, of course, that the representation of the young woman by a bad artist will be more valuable, as a picture, than a composition of circles, squares and triangles devised by a good one. But it does mean, I think, that nature is a richer source of forms than any text-book of plane or solid geometry. Nature has evolved innumerable forms and, as we ourselves move from point to point, we see large numbers of these forms, grouped in an endless variety of ways and thus creating an endless variety of new forms, all of which may be used as the raw materials of works of art. What is given is incomparably richer than what we can invent. But the richness of nature is, from our point of view, a chaos upon which we, as philosophers, men of science, technicians and artists, must impose various kinds of unity. Now, I would say that, other things being equal, a work of art which imposes aesthetic unity upon a large number of formal and psychological elements is a greater and more interesting work than one in which unity is imposed upon only a few elements. In other words, there is a hierarchy of perfections. Bach's Two-Part Inventions are perfect in their way. But his Chromatic Fantasia is also perfect; and since its perfection involves the imposition of aesthetic unity upon a larger number of elements it is (as we all in fact recognize) a greater work. The old distinction between the Fine Arts and the crafts is based to some extent upon snobbery and other non-aesthetic considerations. But not entirely. In the hierarchy of perfections a perfect vase or a perfect carpet occupies a lower rank than that, say, of Giotto's frescoes at Padua, or Rembrandt's *Polish Rider*, or the *Grande Jatte* of Georges Seurat. In these and a hundred other masterpieces of painting the pictorial whole embraces and unifies a repertory of forms much more numerous, varied, strange and interesting than those which come together in the wholes organized by even the most gifted craftsmen. And, over and above this richer and subtler formal perfection, we are presented with a non-pictorial bonus of a story and, explicit or implicit, a criticism of life. At their best, non-representational compositions achieve perfection; but it is a perfection nearer to that of the jug or rug than to that of the enormously complex and yet completely unified masterpieces of representational art—most of which, as we have seen, contain expressive passages of almost pure abstraction. At the present time it would seem that the most sensible and rewarding thing for a painter to do is (like Braque, for example) to make the best and the most of both worlds, representational as well as non-representational.

Within his own Byzantine-Venetian tradition El Greco did precisely this, combining representation with abstraction in a manner which we are accustomed to regard as characteristically modern. His intention, as we have seen, was to use this powerful artistic instrument to express, in visual terms, man's capacity for union with the divine. But the artistic means he employed were such that it was not possible for him to carry out that intention. The existence of a spiritual reality transcendent and yet immanent, absolutely other and yet the sustaining spiritual essence of every being, has frequently been rendered in visual symbols—but not symbols of the kind employed by El Greco. The agitation of quasi-visceral forms in an overcrowded and almost spaceless world from which non-human nature has been banished cannot, in the very nature of things, express man's union with the Spirit who must be worshipped in spirit.

Landscape and the human figure in repose—these are the symbols through which, in the past, the spiritual life has been most clearly and powerfully expressed, 'Be still and know that I am God'. Recollectedness is the indispensable means to the

unitive knowledge of spiritual reality; and though recollectedness should and by some actually can be practised in the midst of
the most violent physical activity, it is most effectively symbolized
by a body in repose and a face that expresses an inner serenity.
The carved or painted Buddhas and Bodhisattvas of India and
the Far East are perhaps the most perfect examples of such visual
symbols of the spiritual life. Hardly less adequate are the majestic
Byzantine figures of Christ, the Virgin and the Saints. It seems
strange that El Greco, who received his first training from
Byzantine masters, should not have recognized the symbolical
value of repose, but should have preferred to represent or,
through his accessory abstractions, to imply, an agitation wholly
incompatible with the spiritual life of which he had read in the
pages of Dionysius.

No less strange is the fact that a disciple of Titian should have
ignored landscape and that a Neo-Platonist should have failed
to perceive that, in the aged master's religious pictures, the only
hint of spirituality was to be found, not in the all too human
figures, but in the backgrounds of Alpine foothills, peaks and
skies. Civilized man spends most of his life in a cosy little universe
of material artefacts, of social conventions and of verbalized
ideas. Only rarely, if he is the inhabitant of a well-ordered
city, does he come into direct contact with the mystery of the
non-human world, does he become aware of modes of being
incommensurable with his own, of vast, indefinite extensions, of
durations all but everlasting. From time immemorial deity has
been associated with the boundlessness of earth and sky, with the
longevity of trees, rivers and mountains, with Leviathan and the
whirlwind, with sunshine and the lilies of the field. Space and
time on the cosmic scale are symbols of the infinity and eternity
of Spirit. Non-human nature is the outward and visible expression of the mystery which confronts us when we look into the
depths of our own being. The first artists to concern themselves
with the spiritual significance of nature were the Taoist landscape painters of China. 'Cherishing the Way, a virtuous man
responds to objects. Clarifying his mind, a wise man appreciates

forms. As to landscapes, they exist in material substance and soar into the realm of spirit. . . . The virtuous man follows the Way by spiritual insight; the wise man takes the same approach. But the lovers of landscape are led into the Way by a sense of form. . . . The significance which is too subtle to be communicated by means of word of mouth may be grasped by the mind through books and writings. Then how much more so in my case, when I have wandered among the rocks and hills and carefully observed them with my own eyes! I render form by form and appearance by appearance. . . . The truth comprises the expression received through the eyes and recognized by the mind. If, in painting, therefore, the likeness of an object is skilfully portrayed, both the eyes and the mind will approve. When the eyes respond and the mind agrees with the objects, the divine spirit may be felt and truth may be attained in the painting.' So wrote Tsung Ping, who was a contemporary of St Augustine, in an Introduction to *Landscape Painting*, which has become a Chinese classic. When, twelve hundred years later, European artists discovered landscape, they developed no philosophy to explain and justify what they were doing. That was left to the poets—to Wordsworth, to Shelley, to Whitman. The Presence which they found in nature, 'the Spirit of each spot', is identical with Hsuan P'in, the mysterious Valley Spirit of the Tao Te Ching, who reveals herself to the landscape painter and, by him, is revealed to others in his pictures. But the lack of an explanatory philosophy did not prevent the best of the European landscape painters from making manifest that

> 'Something far more deeply interfused,
>   Whose dwelling is the light of setting suns,
>   And the round ocean, and the living air,
>   And the blue sky, and in the mind of man.'

'This is not drawing,' Blake exclaimed, when he was shown one of Constable's sketches, 'this is inspiration'. And though Constable himself protested that it was only drawing, the fact remains that the best of his landscapes are powerful and convincing renderings of the spiritual reality in which all things have their being. Indeed, they are much more adequate as symbols of spiritual life than the majority of the works in which Blake consciously tried to express his spiritualist philosophy. Much less gifted as painter than as poet, and brought up in a deplorable artistic tradition, Blake rarely produced a picture that 'comes off' to the extent of expressing what he says so perfectly in his lyrics and in isolated passages of the Prophetic Books. Constable, on the other hand, is a great nature mystic without knowing or intending it. In this he reminds us of Seurat. 'They see poetry in what I do,' complained that consummate master of landscape. 'No; I apply my method and that is all there is to it.' But the method was applied by a painter who combined the most exquisite sensibility with intellectual powers of the first order. Consequently what Seurat supposed to be merely *pointillisme* was in fact inspiration—was a vision of the world in which material reality if the symbol and, one might say, the incarnation of an all-embracing spiritual reality. The famous method was the means whereby he told this Taostic and Wordsworthian story; *pointillisme*, as he used it, permitted him to render empty space as no other painter has ever done, and to impose, through colour, an unprecedented degree of unity upon his composition. In Seurat's paintings the near and the far are separate and yet are one. The emptiness which is the symbol of infinity is of the same substance as the finite forms it contains. The transient participates in the eternal, *samsara* and *nirvana* are one and the same. Such is the poetry with which, in spite of himself, Seurat filled those wonderful landscapes of Honfleur and Gravelines and the Seine. And such is the poetry which El Greco, in spite of what seems to have been a conscious desire to imply it, was forced by the nature of his artistic instrument to exclude from every picture he painted. His peculiar treatment of space and form tells a story of obscure happenings in the sub-conscious mind—of some haunting fear of wide vistas and the open air, some dream of security in the imagined equivalent of a womb. The conscious aspiration towards union with, and perfect freedom in, the divine spirit is overridden by a sub-conscious longing for the consolations of some ineffable uterine state. In these paintings there is no redemption of time by eternity, no trans-figuration of matter by the spirit. On the contrary, it is the low-level organic that has engulfed the spiritual and transformed it into its own substance.

When we think of it in relation to the great world of human experience, El Greco's universe of swallowed spirit and visceral rapture seems, as I have said, curiously oppressive and disquieting. But considered as an isolated artistic system, how strong and coherent it seems, how perfectly unified, how fascinatingly beautiful! And because of this inner harmony and coherence, it asserts in one way all that it had denied in another. El Greco's conscious purpose was to affirm man's capacity for union with the divine. Unconsciously, by his choice of forms and his peculiar treatment of space, he proclaimed the triumph of the organic and the incapacity of spirit, so far as he personally was concerned, to transfigure the matter with which it is associated. But at the same time he was a painter of genius. Out of the visceral forms and cramped spaces, imposed upon him by a part of his being beyond his voluntary control, he was able to create a new kind of order and perfection and, through this order and perfection, to re-affirm the possibility of man's union with the Spirit—a possibility which the raw materials of his pictures had seemed to rule out.

There is no question here of a dialectical process of thesis, antithesis and synthesis. A work of art is not a becoming, but a multiple being. It exists and has significance on several levels at once. In most cases these significances are of the same kind and harmoniously reinforce one another. Not always, however. Occasionally it happens that each of the meanings is logically exclusive of all the rest. There is then a happy marriage of incompatibles, a perfect fusion of contradictions. It is one of those states which, though inconceivable, actually occur. Such things cannot be; and yet, when you enter the Prado, when you visit Toledo, there they actually are.

DOODLES IN THE DICTIONARY

From *Adonis and the Alphabet* (1956)

IN only one respect do I resemble Shakespeare: I know little Latin and less Greek. Once, long ago, I knew quite a lot of both. I had to; for I was brought up in what it is now fashionable to call the Western Tradition, the educational system which equated wisdom with a knowledge of the classical authors in the original, and defined culture as an ability to write grammatically correct Greek and Latin prose. And not merely prose; for at Eton, in my day, we strictly meditated the thankless Muse. The whole of every Tuesday, from seven in the morning until ten at night, was devoted to the exhausting and preposterous task of translating thirty or forty lines of English poetry into Latin or, on great occasions, Greek verses. For those who were most successful in producing pastiches of Ovid or Horace or Euripides, there were handsome prizes. I still have a Matthew Arnold in crimson morocco, a Shelley in half-calf, to testify to my one-time prowess in these odd fields of endeavour. Today I could no more write a copy of Greek iambics, or even of Latin hexameters, than I could fly. All I can remember of these once indispensable arts is the intense boredom by which the practice of them was accompanied. Even today the sight of Dr Smith's Shorter Latin Dictionary, or of Liddell's and Scott's Greek Lexicon, has power to recall that ancient ennui. What dreary hours I have spent frantically turning those pages in search of a word for 'cow' that could be scanned as a dactyl, or to make sure that my memory of the irregular verbs and the Greek accents was not at fault! I hate to think of all that wasted time. And yet, in view of the fact that most human beings are destined to pass most of their lives at jobs in which it is impossible for them to take the slightest interest, this old-fashioned training with the dictionary may have been extremely salutary. At least it taught one to know and expect the worst of life. Whereas the pupil in a progressive school, where everything is made to seem entertaining and significant, lives in a fool's paradise. As a preparation for life, not as it ought to be, but as it actually is, the horrors of Greek grammar and the systematic idiocy of Latin Verses were perfectly appropriate. On the other hand, it must be admitted that they tended to leave their victims with a quite irrational distate for poor dear Dr Smith.

Not long ago, for example, I had an urgent call from my friend Jake Zeitlin, the bookseller .'I have something to show you,' he said, 'something very exciting.' I walked over to his shop without delay. But when, triumphantly, he held up a small Latin dictionary, my heart sank and I found myself feeling—such is the force of the conditioned reflex—some of the weariness of spirit which such objects had evoked during my schooldays, nearly half a century ago. True, this particular dictionary was the work of an Agrégé des Classes de Grammaire des Lycées, and the equivalents of the Latin words were in French. But the resemblance to Dr Smith was sufficiently close to trigger my customary reaction. Looking at it, I felt all of a sudden like one who has just inhaled a lungful of stale air at the entrance to a subway station. But then the book was opened and reverently laid before me. On the almost blank fly-leaf was an exquisite pen-and-ink drawing of three horses in tandem straining on the traces of a heavy two-wheeled cart. It was a marvel of expressiveness, of truth to nature, of economy of means. How had this lovely thing found its way into the dismal counterpart of Shorter Smith? The answer, when it came, was as simple as it was surprising. This dictionary had belonged, in the late seventies and earliest eighties of the last century, to a boy called Henri de Toulouse-Lautrec.

In 1880, when most of these drawings were made, Toulouse-Lautrec was sixteen. The first of the two accidents, which were to transform a merely delicate child into a grotesquely deformed cripple, had taken place in the spring of 1878; the second, fifteen months later, in the late summer of 1879. By 1880 the broken thigh bones had mended, more or less; and he still believed—to judge from the pictures he drew of himself at this time—that his legs would start growing again. He was mistaken. His trunk developed normally and became in due course the torso of an adult man; the legs remained what they had been at the time of his first fall, the short, spindly shanks of a boy of fourteen. Meanwhile life had to be lived; and in spite of pain, in spite of enforced inactivity, in spite of the suspicion and then the certainty that he henceforward had to face the world as a dwarfish monster, Lautrec lived it with unfailing courage and irrepressible high spirits. His education, interrupted after less than three years at the Lycée, was carried on under private tutors and in 1880 he sat for his baccalaureate examination, failed, took the test again in 1881 and came through with flying colours. It was in the interval between the two examinations that he decorated the margins of his dictionary with the drawings at which I was now looking, entranced, in Jake Zeitlin's shop.

Up to the age of ten (provided of course that his teachers don't interfere) practically every child paints like a genius. Fifteen years later the chance of his still painting like a genius are about four hundred thousand to one. Why this infinitesimal minority should fulfil the promise of childhood, while all the rest either dwindle into mediocrity or forget the very existence of the art they once practised (within the limits of childish capacity) with such amazing skill and originality, is an unsolved riddle. When we have learned its answer, we may be able to transform education from the sadly disappointing affair it now is into the instrument of social and individual reconstruction which it ought to be. Meanwhile we can only record the facts without understanding them. For some as yet entirely mysterious reason, Lautrec was one of the infinitesimal minority. His interest in painting began very early, and along with it, presumably, went the ordinary childish genius. At three, it is recorded, he asked to be allowed to sign the parish register on the occasion of his baby brother's christening. It was objected, not unreasonably, that he didn't know how to write. 'Very well,' he answered, 'I will draw an ox.' Throughout his childhood oxen remained a favourite subject; and along with oxen, dogs, poultry, falcons (his father, Count Alphonse de Toulouse-Lautrec, was a passionate falconer), and above all horses. He would spend long hours in the barnyard of one or other of the family châteaux, gazing intently at the birds and animals. And what he saw he remembered, not vaguely and imprecisely as the rest of us remember things, but in all its detail. And later, when the imaginative and symbolic art of childhood gave place to his first adolescent essays in representation, he was able to reproduce these memories with amazing precision. Later, as a mature artist, he seldom used models; he preferred to rely on a memory which could supply him with everything he needed. Is this kind of memory inborn, or can it be acquired by suitable training? Are we all capable of accurate recall, and do we fail to realize our innate potentialities because of some improper use of our minds and bodies? Here is another riddle which educators might profitably investigate.

Lautrec was good at Latin and in the course of his three years at school carried off several prizes for composition and translation. But proficiency did not exclude boredom, and when the learned foolery of grammar and versification became unbearable, he would open the equivalent of Shorter Smith, dip his pen in the ink and draw a tiny masterpiece. *Dictionnaire Latin-Français*. Above the words is a cavalryman galloping to the left, a jockey walking his horse towards the right. We open the book at random and find *Prophetice*, *Propheticus* with a falcon alighting on them. *Coetus* and *Cohaerentia* are topped by a pair of horse's hoofs, glimpsed from the back as the animal canters past. Two pages of the preface are made beautiful, the first by an unusually large drawing of a tired old nag, the second by another and no less powerful version of the three horses in tandem, which adorned the fly-leaf.

The draughtsman was only sixteen; but these furtive doodlings, while his tutor's back was turned, are the works of an already mature artist, and exhibit an easy mastery of the medium and an understanding of the subject matter which, in the case even of most men of outstanding talent, are the fruit only of long experience and constant practice. Lautrec's first master, the academician and fashionable portrait painter, Bonnat, was of another opinion. 'Perhaps you are curious to know,' the boy wrote in a letter to his Uncle Charles, 'what sort of encouragement I am getting from Bonnat. He tells me: "Your painting isn't bad; it's clever, but still it isn't bad. But your drawing is simply atrocious".' This to a pupil who could scribble from memory little things of which even the greatest master would not feel ashamed! The reason for Bonnat's disapproval becomes clear when we read what a fellow-student wrote of Lautrec in the life class. 'He made a great effort to copy the model exactly; but in spite of himself he exaggerated certain typical details, sometimes the general character, so that he distorted without trying to or even wanting to. I have seen him forcing himself to 'prettify' his study of a model—in my opinion, without success. The expression "*se forcer à faire joli*" is his own.'

The word 'fact' is derived from *factum*, 'something made'. And in fact, a fact is never, as we like to suppose, a wholly independent, given thing, but always what we choose to make of that given thing. A fact is that particular version of the given which, in any particular context, we find useful. The same event, say the explosion of an H-bomb, is simultaneously a fact in the sphere of physics and chemistry, a fact in physiology, medicine and genetics, a psychological fact, a political fact, an economic fact, an ethical fact, even an aesthetic fact—for the atomic cloud is wonderfully beautiful. A great representational artist, such as Lautrec or Goya, as Degas or Rembrandt, is interested in several aspects of experience—the aesthetic, the biological, the psychological and, sometimes, the ethical—and the facts which he sets down on paper or canvas are forms which he extracts from given reality, which he *makes*, for the purpose of expressing and communicating his own special preoccupations. For this reason he finds no incompatibility between truth to nature and distortion. Indeed, if there is to be truth to the particular aspects of nature in which he is interested, there must be a certain amount of distortion. Sometimes the distortion is mainly a matter of omission. (Few even of the most realistic painters portray *every* eyelash.) Sometimes it is due to an exaggeration of that which, in the given, reveals most clearly the side of Nature to which the artist aspires to be true. Hsieh Ho, the fourth-century artist who formulated the famous Six Principles of Chinese painting, expressed the same truth in another way. 'The first principle is that, through a vitalizing spirit, a painting should possess the movement of life.' A number of other renderings of the First Principle have been suggested, such as 'a painting should possess rhythmic vitality'; 'a painting should express the life movement of the spirit through the rhythm of things'; 'a painting should manifest the fusion of the rhythm of the spirit with the movement of living things.' But, however the renderings may vary, 'it is quite evident', in the words of the great Sinologist, Osvald Siren, 'that the First Principle refers to something beyond the material form, call it character, soul, or expression. It depends on the operation of the spirit, or the mysterious breath of life, by which the figures may become as though they were moving or breathing.' It is to this rhythm of the spirit manifested by the movement of given events that the artist pays attention; and in order to render this spiritual essence of things, he may be compelled to distort appearance, to refrain both from exactly copying or conventionally prettifying. In his own way Lautrec was a faithful exponent of Hsieh Ho's First Principle. Even as a boy, as yet completely ignorant of the masters under whose influence his mature style was to be formed, Hokusai, Degas, Goya, even in the margins of his Latin dictionary he was making manifest the vitalizing spirit in the movements of life.

The horse is now an almost extinct animal and in a few years, I suppose, will be seen only in zoos and, perhaps, on race tracks and in the parks of Texas oil millionaires. For the man in the street—a street now blessedly undefiled by the mountains of dung which, in my childhood, used to make of every metropolis an Augean stable—the disappearance of the horse is a blessing. For the budding artist, it is a disaster. The percheron, the thorough-bred hunter, the sleek cob, the splendid creatures that drew the rich man's carriage, even the miserable hacks in the shafts of cabs and omnibuses—each in its own way manifestly embodied the rhythm of the spirit in the movement of its equine life. Today, in the great cities of Europe and America, the movement of life is confined to human beings, most of whom are incredibly grace-less, and to a few dogs, cats and starlings. Communications are assured (and at the same time obstructed) by automobiles. But automobiles completely lack the movement of life. They are static objects fitted with a motor. To make them look as though they had the movement of life, their manufacturers give them inconvenient shapes and decorate them with arrowy strips of chromium. But it is all in vain. The most rakish sports car remains, even at a hundred miles an hour, essentially undynamic. Whereas even at five miles an hour, even a cab horse is a mani-festation of life movement, an embodiment of the rhythm of the spirit. In the past, the horse was ubiquitous. Wherever he turned the young artist saw life movement. Walking or trotting, canter-ing or galloping, it challenged his powers of representation and expression, it spurred him to explore the underlying mystery of the spirit which lives and moves in forms. What amazing works of art have owed their existence to the horse! In ancient Meso-potamia, in Greece, in China and Japan, among the Etruscans and at Rome, in the battle pictures of the Renaissance, in scores of paintings by Rubens, by Velasquez, by Géricault, by Dela-croix—what a cavalcade! The invention of the internal-combus-tion engine has deprived the painters and sculptors of the twentieth century of one of the richest sources of artistic inspira-tion. Along with Degas, Lautrec was almost the last of the great portrayers of horses. Indeed, if Count Alphonse had had his way, Henri would never have painted anything else. 'This little book', wrote the Count on the fly-leaf of a manual of falconry pre-sented to his son when he was twelve, 'will teach you to enjoy the life of the great outdoors, and if one day you should experi-ence the bitterness of life, dogs and falcons and, above all, horses will be your faithful companions and will help you to forget a little.' And it is not only the bitterness of human life, it is also its appalling vulgarity that dogs and falcons and horses will help us forget. This, surely, is why Disney's nature films have achieved so wide a popularity. After an overdose of all too human hams, what an enormous relief to see even a tarantula, even a pair of scorpions! But, alas, life in the great outdoors was not the life which fate had prepared for Henri de Toulouse-Lautrec. His accident debarred him from participation in any form of sport or country exercise. And though he still loved horses and was never tired of studying their life-movements at the circus and on the race track, he loved Montmartre and alcohol, cabaret singers and prostitutes with an even intenser passion. 'Any curiosity,' wrote one of his friends, 'delighted him, stirred him to joyful enthusiasm. He would fish out such odds and ends as a Japanese wig, a ballet slipper, a peculiar hat, a shoe with an exaggeratedly high heel and show them to you with the most amusing remarks; or else he would unexpectedly turn up, in the pile of debris, a fine Hokusai print, a letter written by a pimp to his mistress, a set of photographs of such splendid masterpieces of painting as Uccello's *Battle* in the National Gallery, or Carpaccio's *Courtesans playing with Animals* in the Correr Museum, all of which he accompanied by enthusiastic exclamations and sensitive or explosive comments.' The drunks and tarts, the lecherous gentlemen in top hats, the sensation-hunting ladies in feather boas, the stable boys, the lesbians, the bearded surgeons performing operations with a horrifying disregard of the first principles of asepsis—these also were curiosities, more remarkable even than Japanese wigs, and these became the subject matter of most of Lautrec's pictures, the environment in which he liked to live. He portrayed them simply as curiosities, passing no moral judgment, but simply rendering the intrinsic oddity of what he saw around him. It was in this spirit of the curiosity hunter, the collector of odds and ends that he visited the theatre. Plays as such did not interest him. Good or bad, they were merely strings of words. What he liked in a theatre was not the literature, but the actors—the way they grimaced and gesticulated, the curious effects produced by the lights from above and beneath, the garish costumes moving against preposterously romantic backgrounds of painted canvas. The first beginnings of this interest in the theatre are visible in Lautrec's dictionary. Above *pugillus*, there is a diminutive jester in cap and bells—a memory, presumably, of some figure seen during the carnival at Nice. And encroaching upon *quamprimum, quamquam, quamvis* and *quanam* is a personage whose attitude and vaguely mediaeval costume would seem to be those of an actor in one of the touring companies which Henri may have seen on the Riviera. And finally, opposite *Naenia* (the word for 'funeral chant'), there is a beautiful sketch of a young actress dressed as a page in tights (for legs were not bared until well after the First World War), the briefest of trunk hose and a doublet. There is no effort in this or any other drawing by the youthful Lautrec to stress the feminity of his model. Our current obsession with the bosom is conspicuously absent. Generally speaking, hope springs eternal in the male breast in regard to the female breast. Here there is no undue optimism. In Lautrec, the clear-sighted artist is stronger than the yearning adolescent, as it was to be stronger, later on, than the frequenter of brothels. There is never anything sexy about Lautrec's art; but there also is never anything deliberately, sarcastically anti-feminist in it. Degas, it is evident, took pleasure in posing his models in the most unalluring postures. A lady who had visited an exhibition of his works once asked him why he chose to make all his women look so ugly. 'Madame', the painter replied, 'because women generally *are* ugly.' Unlike Degas, Lautrec never set out to prove that they were either ugly or attractive. He just looked at them, as he had looked from his earliest childhood at oxen, horses, falcons, dogs, then, from memory and with appropriate distortions, rendered their life-movement, now graceful, now grotesque, and the underlying rhythm of the mysterious spirit that manifests itself within that movement.

OVERPOPULATION

From *Brave New World Revisited* (1959)

IN 1931, when *Brave New World* was being written, I was convinced that there was still plenty of time. The completely organized society, the scientific caste system, the abolition of free will by methodical conditioning, the servitude made acceptable by regular doses of chemically induced happiness, the orthodoxies drummed in by nightly courses of sleep-teaching—these things were coming all right, but not in my time, not even in the time of my grandchildren. I forget the exact date of the events recorded in *Brave New World*; but it was somewhere in the sixth or seventh century A.F. (after Ford). We who were living in the second quarter of the twentieth century A.D. were the inhabitants admittedly, of a gruesome kind of universe; but the nightmare of those depression years was radically different from the nightmare of the future, described in *Brave New World*. Ours was a nightmare of too little order; theirs, in the seventh century A.F., of too much. In the process of passing from one extreme to the other, there would be a long interval, so I imagined, during which the more fortunate third of the human race would make the best of both worlds—the disorderly world of liberalism and the much too orderly Brave New World where perfect efficiency left no room for freedom or personal initiative.

Twenty-seven years later, in this third quarter of the twentieth century A.D., and long before the end of the first century A.F., I feel a good deal less optimistic than I did when I was writing *Brave New World*. The prophecies made in 1931 are coming true much sooner than I thought they would. The blessed interval between too little order and the nightmare of too much has not begun and shows no sign of beginning. In the West, it is true, individual men and women still enjoy a large measure of freedom. But even in those countries that have a tradition of democratic government, this freedom and even the desire for this freedom seem to be on the wane. In the rest of the world freedom for individuals has already gone, or is manifestly about to go. The nightmare of total organization, which I had situated in the seventh century after Ford, has emerged from the safe, remote future and is now awaiting us, just around the next corner.

George Orwell's *1984* was a magnified projection into the future of a present that contained Stalinism and an immediate past that had witnessed the flowering of Nazism. *Brave New World* was written before the rise of Hitler to supreme power in Germany and when the Russian tyrant had not yet got into his stride. In 1931 systematic terrorism was not the obsessive contemporary fact which it had become in 1948, and the future dictatorship of my imaginary world was a good deal less brutal than the future dictatorship so brilliantly portrayed by Orwell. In the context of 1948, *1984* seemed dreadfully convincing. But tyrants, after all, are mortal and circumstances change. Recent developments in Russia, and recent advances in science and technology, have robbed Orwell's book of some of its gruesome verisimilitude. A nuclear war will, of course, make nonsense of everybody's predictions. But, assuming for the moment that the Great Powers can somehow refrain from destroying us, we can say that it now looks as though the odds were more in favour of something like *Brave New World* than of something like *1984*.

In the light of what we have recently learned about animal behaviour in general, and human behaviour in particular, it has become clear that control through the punishment of undesirable behaviour is less effective, in the long run, than control through the reinforcement of desirable behaviour by rewards, and that government through terror works on the whole less well than government through the non-violent manipulation of the environment and of the thoughts and feelings of individual men, women and children. Punishment temporarily puts a stop to undesirable behaviour, but does not permanently reduce the victim's tendency to indulge in it. Moreover, the psycho-physical by-products of punishment may be just as undesirable as the behaviour for which an individual has been punished. Psycho-therapy is largely concerned with the debilitating or anti-social consequences of past punishments.

The society described in *1984* is a society controlled almost exclusively by punishment and the fear of punishment. In the imaginary world of my own fable, punishment is infrequent and generally mild. The nearly perfect control exercised by the government is achieved by systematic reinforcement of desirable behaviour, by many kinds of nearly non-violent manipulation, both physical and psychological, and by genetic standardization. Babies in bottles and the centralized control of reproduction are not perhaps impossible; but it is quite clear that for a long time to come we shall remain a viviparous species breeding at random. For practical purposes genetic standardization may be ruled out. Societies will continue to be controlled post-natally—by punishment, as in the past, and to an ever-increasing extent by the more effective methods of reward and scientific manipulation.

In Russia the old-fashioned, *1984*-style dictatorship of Stalin has begun to give way to a more up-to-date form of tyranny. In the upper levels of the Soviets' hierarchical society the reinforcement of desirable behaviour has begun to replace the older methods of control through the punishment of undesirable behaviour. Engineers and scientists, teachers and administrators, are handsomely paid for good work and so moderately taxed that they are under a constant incentive to do better and so be more highly rewarded. In certain areas they are at liberty to think and do more or less what they like. Punishment awaits them only when they stray beyond their prescribed limits into the realms of ideology and politics. It is because they have been granted a measure of professional freedom that Russian teachers, scientists and technicians have achieved such remarkable successes. Those who live near the base of the Soviet pyramid enjoy none of the privileges accorded to the lucky or specially gifted minority. Their wages are meagre and they pay, in the form of high prices, a disproportionately large share of the taxes. The area in which they can do as they please is extremely restricted, and their rulers control them more by punishment and the threat of punishment than through non-violent manipulation or the reinforcement of desirable behaviour by reward. The Soviet system combines elements of *1984* with elements that are prophetic of what went on among the higher castes in *Brave New World*.

Meanwhile impersonal forces over which we have almost no control seem to be pushing us all in the direction of the Brave New Worldian nightmare; and this impersonal pushing is being consciously accelerated by representatives of commercial and political organizations who have developed a number of new techniques for manipulating, in the interests of some minority, the thoughts and feelings of the masses. The techniques of manipulation will be discussed in later chapters. For the moment let us confine our attention to those impersonal forces which are now making the world so extremely unsafe for democracy, so very inhospitable to individual freedom. What are these forces? And why has the nightmare, which I had projected into the seventh century A.F., made so swift an advance in our direction? The answer to these questions must begin where the life of even the most highly civilized society has its beginnings—on the level of biology.

On the first Christmas Day the population of our planet was about two hundred and fifty millions—less than half the population of modern China. Sixteen centuries later, when the Pilgrim Fathers landed at Plymouth Rock, human numbers had climbed to a little more than five hundred millions. By the time of the signing of the Declaration of Independence, world population had passed the seven hundred million mark. In 1931, when I was writing *Brave New World*, it stood at just under two billions. Today, only twenty-seven years later, there are two thousand eight hundred million of us. And tomorrow—what? Penicillin, DDT and clean water are cheap commodities, whose effects on public health are out of all proportion to their cost. Even the poorest government is rich enough to provide its subjects with a substantial measure of death control. Birth control is a very different matter. Death control is something which can be provided for a whole people by a few technicians working in the pay of a benevolent government. Birth control depends on the co-operation of an entire people. It must be practised by countless individuals, from whom it demands more intelligence and will power than most of the world's teeming illiterates possess, and (where chemical or mechanical methods of contraception are used) an expenditure of more money than most of these millions can now afford. Moreover, there are nowhere any religious traditions in favour of unrestricted death, whereas religious and social traditions in favour of unrestricted reproduction are widespread. For all these reasons, death control is achieved very easily, birth control is achieved with great difficulty. Death rates have therefore fallen in recent years with startling suddenness. But birth rates have either remained at their old high level or, if they have fallen, have fallen very little and at a very slow rate. In consequence, human numbers are now increasing more rapidly than at any time in the history of the species.

Moreover, the yearly increases are themselves increasing. They increase regularly, according to the rules of compound interest; and they also increase irregularly with every application, by a technologically backward society, of the principles of Public Health. At the present time the annual increase in world population runs to about forty-three millions. This means that every four years mankind adds to its numbers the equivalent of the present population of the United States, every eight and a half years the equivalent of the present population of India. At the rate of increase prevailing between the birth of Christ and the death of Queen Elizabeth I it took sixteen centuries for the population of the earth to double. At the present rate it will double in less than half a century. And this fantastically rapid doubling of our numbers will be taking place on a planet whose most desirable and productive areas are already densely populated, whose soils are being eroded by the frantic efforts of bad farmers to raise more food, and whose easily available mineral capital is being squandered with the reckless extravagance of a drunken sailor getting rid of his accumulated pay.

In the Brave New World of my fable, the problem of human numbers in their relation to natural resources had been effectively solved. An optimum figure for world population had been calculated and numbers were maintained at this figure (a little under two billions, if I remember rightly) generation after generation. In the real contemporary world, the population problem has not been solved. On the contrary it is becoming graver and more formidable with every passing year. It is against this grim biological background that all the political, economic, cultural and psychological dramas of our time are being played out. As the twentieth century wears on, as the new billions are added to the existing billions (there will be more than five and a half billions of us by the time my granddaughter is fifty), this biological background will advance, ever more insistently, ever more menacingly, towards the front and centre of the historical stage. The problem of rapidly increasing numbers in relation to natural resources, to social stability and to the well-being of individuals—this is now the central problem of mankind; and it will remain the central problem certainly for another century, and perhaps for several centuries thereafter. A new age is supposed to have begun on October 4th 1957. But actually, in the present context, all our exuberant post-Sputnik talk is irrelevant and even nonsensical. So far as the masses of mankind are concerned, the coming time will not be the Space Age; it will be the Age of Overpopulation. We can parody the words of the old song and ask,

> Will the space that you're so rich in
> Light a fire in the kitchen,
> Or the little god of space turn the spit, spit, spit?

The answer, it is obvious, is in the negative. A settlement on the moon may be of some military advantage to the nation that does the settling. But it will do nothing whatever to make life more tolerable, during the fifty years that it will take our present population to double, for the earth's undernourished and proliferating billions. And even if, at some future date, emigration to Mars should become feasible, even if any considerable number of men and women were desperate enough to choose a new life under conditions comparable to those prevailing on a mountain twice as high as Mount Everest, what difference would that make? In the course of the last four centuries quite a number of people sailed from the Old World to the New. But neither their departure nor the returning flow of food and raw materials could solve the problems of the Old World. Similarly the shipping of a few surplus humans to Mars (at a cost, for transportation and development, of several million dollars a head) will do nothing to solve the problem of mounting population pressures on our own planet. Unsolved, that problem will render insoluble all our other problems. Worse still, it will create conditions in which individual freedom and the social decencies of the democratic way of life will become impossible, almost unthinkable.

Not all dictatorships arise in the same way. There are many roads to Brave New World; but perhaps the straightest and the broadest of them is the road we are travelling today, the road that leads through gigantic numbers and accelerating increases. Let us briefly review the reasons for this close correlation between too many people, too rapidly multiplying, and the formulation of authoritarian philosophies, the rise of totalitarian systems of government.

As large and increasing numbers press more heavily upon available resources, the economic position of the society undergoing this ordeal becomes ever more precarious. This is especially true of those underdeveloped regions, where a sudden lowering of the death rate by means of DDT, penicillin and clean water has not been accompanied by a corresponding fall in the birth rate. In parts of Asia and in most of Central and South America populations are increasing so fast that they will double themselves in little more than twenty years. If the production of food and manufactured articles, of houses, schools and teachers, could be increased at a greater rate than human numbers, it would be possible to improve the wretched lot of those who live in these underdeveloped and overpopulated countries. But unfortunately these countries lack not merely agricultural machinery and an industrial plant capable of turning out this machinery, but also the capital required to create such a plant. Capital is what is left over after the primary needs of a population have been satisfied. But the primary needs of most of the people in underdeveloped countries are never fully satisfied. At the end of each year almost nothing is left over, and there is therefore almost no capital available for creating the industrial and agricultural plant, by means of which the people's needs might be satisfied. Moreover, there is, in all these underdeveloped countries, a serious shortage of the trained manpower without which a modern industrial and agricultural plant cannot be operated. The present educational facilities are inadequate; so are the resources, financial and cultural, for improving the existing facilities as fast as the situation demands. Meanwhile the population of some of these underdeveloped countries is increasing at the rate of three per cent per annum.

Their tragic situation is discussed in an important book, published in 1957—*The Next Hundred Years*, by Professors Harrison Brown, James Bonner and John Weir of the California Institute of Technology. How is mankind coping with the problem of rapidly increasing numbers? Not very successfully. "The evidence suggests rather strongly that in most underdeveloped countries the lot of the average individual has worsened appreciably in the last half-century. People have become more poorly fed. There are fewer available goods per person. And practically every attempt to improve the situation has been nullified by the relentless pressure of continued population growth.'

Whenever the economic life of a nation becomes precarious, the central government is forced to assume additional responsibilities for the general welfare. It must work out elaborate plans for dealing with a critical situation; it must impose ever greater restrictions upon the activities of its subjects; and if, as is very likely, worsening economic conditions result in political unrest, or open rebellion, the central government must intervene to preserve public order and its own authority. More and more power is thus concentrated in the hands of the executives and their bureaucratic managers. But the nature of power is such that even those who have not sought it, but have had it forced upon them, tend to acquire a taste for more. 'Lead us not into temptation', we pray—and with good reason; for when human beings are tempted too enticingly or too long, they generally yield. A democratic constitution is a device for preventing the local rulers from yielding to those particularly dangerous temptations that arise when too much power is concentrated in too few hands. Such a constitution works pretty well where, as in Britain or the United States, there is a traditional respect for constitutional procedures. Where the republican or limited monarchical tradition is weak, the best of constitutions will not prevent ambitious politicians from succumbing with glee and gusto to the temptations of power. And in any country where numbers have begun to press heavily upon available resources, these temptations cannot fail to arise. Overpopulation leads to economic insecurity and social unrest. Unrest and insecurity lead to more control by central governments and an increase of their power. In the absence of a constitutional tradition, this increased power will probably be exercised in a dictatorial fashion. Even if Communism had never been invented, this would be likely to happen. But Communism has been invented. Given this fact, the probability of overpopulation leading through unrest to dictatorship becomes a virtual certainty. It is a pretty safe bet that, twenty years from now, all the world's overpopulated and underdeveloped countries will be under some form of totalitarian rule—probably by the Communist Party.

How will this development affect the overpopulated, but highly industrialized and still democratic countries of Europe? If the newly formed dictatorships were hostile to them, and if the normal flow of raw materials from the underdeveloped countries were deliberately interrupted, the nations of the West would find themselves in a very bad way indeed. Their industrial system would break down, and the highly developed technology, which up till now has permitted them to sustain a population much greater than that which could be supported by locally available resources, would no longer protect them against the consequences of having too many people in too small a territory. If this should happen, the enormous powers forced by unfavourable conditions upon central governments may come to be used in the spirit of totalitarian dictatorship.

The United States is not at present an overpopulated country. If, however, the population continues to increase at the present rate (which is higher than that of India's increase, though happily a good deal lower than the rate now current in Mexico or Guatemala), the problem of numbers in relation to available resources might well become troublesome by the beginning of the twenty-first century. For the moment overpopulation is not a direct threat to the personal freedom of Americans. It remains, however, an indirect threat, a menace at one remove. If overpopulation should drive the underdeveloped countries into totalitarianism, and if these new dictatorships should ally themselves with Russia, then the military position of the United States would become less secure and the preparations for defence and retaliation would have to be intensified. But liberty, as we all know, cannot flourish in a country that is permanently on a war footing, or even a near-war footing. Permanent crisis justifies permanent control of everybody and everything by the agencies of the central government. And permanent crisis is what we have to expect in a world in which overpopulation is producing a state of things in which dictatorship under Communist auspices becomes almost inevitable.

THE ARTS OF SELLING

From *Brave New World Revisited* (1959)

THE survival of democracy depends on the ability of large numbers of people to make realistic choices in the light of adequate information. A dictatorship, on the other hand, maintains itself by censoring or distorting the facts, and by appealing, not to reason, not to enlightened self-interest, but to passion and prejudice, to the powerful 'hidden forces', as Hitler called them, present in the unconscious depths of every human mind.

In the West, democratic principles are proclaimed and many able and conscientious publicists do their best to supply electors with adequate information and to persuade them, by rational argument, to make realistic choices in the light of that information. All this is greatly to the good. But unfortunately propaganda in the Western democracies, above all in America, has two faces and a divided personality. In charge of the editorial department there is often a democratic Dr Jekyll—a propagandist who would be very happy to prove that John Dewey had been right about the ability of human nature to respond to truth and reason. But this worthy man controls only a part of the machinery of mass communication. In charge of advertising we find an antidemocratic, because anti-rational, Mr Hyde—or rather a Doctor Hyde, for Hyde is now a Ph.D. in psychology and has a master's degree as well in the Social Sciences. This Dr Hyde would be very unhappy indeed if everybody always lived up to John Dewey's faith in human nature. Truth and reason are Jekyll's affair, not his. Hyde is a Motivation Analyst, and his business is to study human weaknesses and failings, to investigate those unconscious desires and fears by which so much of men's conscious thinking and overt doing is determined. And he does this, not in the spirit of the moralist who would like to make people better, or of the physician who would like to improve their health, but simply in order to find out the best way to take advantage of their ignorance and to exploit their irrationality for the pecuniary benefit of his employers. But after all, it may be argued, 'capitalism is dead, consumerism is king'—and consumerism requires the services of expert salesmen versed in all the arts (including the more insidious arts) of persuasion. Under a free enterprise system commercial propaganda by any and every means is absolutely indispensable. But the indispensable is not necessarily the desirable. What is demonstrably good in the sphere of economics may be far from good for men and women as voters or even as human beings. An earlier, more moralistic generation would have been profoundly shocked by the bland cynicism of the Motivation Analysts. Today we read a book like Mr Vance Packard's *The Hidden Persuaders*, and are more amused than horrified, more resigned than indignant. Given Freud, given Behaviourism, given the mass producer's chronically desperate need for mass consumption, this is the sort of thing that is only to be expected. But what, we may ask, is the sort of thing that is to be expected in the future? Are Hyde's activities compatible in the long run with Jekyll's? Can a campaign in favour of rationality be successful in the teeth of another and even more vigorous campaign in favour of irrationality? These are questions which, for the moment, I shall not attempt to answer, but shall leave hanging, so to speak, as a backdrop to our discussion of the methods of mass persuasion in a technologically advanced democratic society.

The task of the commercial propagandist in a democracy is in some ways easier and in some ways more difficult than that of a political propagandist employed by an established dictator or a dictator in the making. It is easier in as much as almost everyone starts out with a prejudice in favour of beer, cigarettes and refrigerators, whereas almost nobody starts out with a prejudice in favour of tyrants. It is more difficult in as much as the commercial propagandist is not permitted, by the rules of his particular game, to appeal to the more savage instincts of his public. The advertiser of dairy products would dearly love to tell his readers and listeners that all their troubles are caused by the machinations of a gang of godless international margarine manufacturers, and that it is their patriotic duty to march out and burn the oppressors' factories. This sort of thing, however, is ruled out, and he must be content with a milder approach. But the mild approach is less exciting than the approach through verbal or physical violence. In the long run, anger and hatred are self-defeating emotions. But in the short run they pay high dividends in the form of psychological and even (since they release large quantities of adrenalin and noradrenalin) physiological satisfaction. People may start out with an initial prejudice against tyrants; but when tyrants or would-be tyrants treat them to adrenalin-releasing propaganda about the wickedness of their enemies—particularly of enemies weak enough to be persecuted —they are ready to follow him with enthusiasm. In his speeches Hitler kept repeating such words as 'hatred', 'force', 'ruthless', 'crush', 'smash'; and he would accompany these violent words with even more violent gestures. He would yell, he would scream, his veins would swell, his face would turn purple. Strong emotion (as every actor and dramatist knows) is in the highest degree contagious. Infected by the malignant frenzy of the orator, the audience would groan and sob and scream in an orgy of uninhibited passion. And these orgies were so enjoyable that most of those who had experienced them eagerly came back for more. Almost all of us long for peace and freedom; but very few of us have much enthusiasm for the thoughts, feelings and actions that make for peace and freedom. Conversely, almost nobody wants war or tyranny; but a great many people find an intense pleasure in the thoughts, feelings and action that make for war and tyranny. These thoughts, feelings and actions are too dangerous to be exploited for commercial purposes. Accepting this handicap, the advertising man must do the best he can with the less intoxicating emotions, the quieter forms of irrationality.

Effective rational propaganda becomes possible only when there is a clear understanding, on the part of all concerned, of the nature of symbols and of their relations to the things and events symbolized. Irrational propaganda depends for its effectiveness on a general failure to understand the nature of symbols. Simple-minded people tend to equate the symbol with what it stands for, to attribute to things and events some of the qualities expressed by the words in terms of which the propagandist has chosen, for his own purposes, to talk about them. Consider a simple example. Most cosmetics are made of lanolin, which is a mixture of purified wool-fat and water beaten up into an emulsion. This emulsion has many valuable properties: it penetrates the skin, it does not become rancid, it is mildly antiseptic, and so forth. But the commercial propagandists do not speak about the genuine virtues of the emulsion. They give it some picturesquely volup-tuous name, talk ecstatically and misleadingly about feminine beauty, and show pictures of gorgeous blondes nourishing their tissues with skin food. 'The cosmetic manufacturers', one of their number has written, 'are not selling lanolin, they are selling hope'. For this hope, this fraudulent implication of a promise that they will be transfigured, women will pay ten or twenty times the value of the emulsion which the propagandists have so skilfully related, by means of misleading symbols, to a deep-seated and almost universal feminine wish—the wish to be more attractive to members of the opposite sex. The principles under-lying this kind of propaganda are extremely simple. Find some common desire, some wide-spread unconscious fear or anxiety; think out some way to relate this wish or fear to the product you have to sell; then, build a bridge of verbal or pictorial symbols over which your customer can pass from fact to compensatory dream, and from the dream to the illusion that your product, when purchased, will make the dream come true. 'We no longer buy oranges, we buy vitality. We do not buy just a car, we buy prestige.' And so with all the rest. In toothpaste, for example, we buy, not a mere cleanser and antiseptic, but release from the fear of being sexually repulsive. In vodka and whisky we are not buying a protoplasmic poison which, in small doses, may depress the nervous system in a psychologically valuable way; we are buying friendliness and good fellowship, the warmth of Dingley Dell and the brilliance of the Mermaid Tavern. With our laxatives we buy the health of a Greek god, the radiance of one of Diana's nymphs. With the monthly best seller we acquire culture, the envy of our less literate neighbours and the respect of the sophisticated. In every case the motivation analyst has found some deep-seated wish or fear, whose energy can be used to move the consumer to part with cash and so, indirectly, to turn the wheels of industry. Stored in the minds and bodies of countless individuals, this potential energy is released by, and transmitted along, a line of symbols carefully laid out so as to by-pass rationality and obscure the real issue.

Sometimes the symbols take effect by being disproportionately impressive, haunting and fascinating in their own right. Of this kind are the rites and pomps of religion. These 'beauties of holiness' strengthen faith where it already exists and, where there is no faith, contribute to conversion. Appealing, as they do, only to the aesthetic sense, they guarantee neither the truth nor the ethical value of the doctrines with which they have been, quite arbitrarily, associated. As a matter of plain historical fact, the beauties of holiness have often been matched and indeed surpassed by the beauties of unholiness. Under Hitler, for example, the yearly Nuremberg rallies were masterpieces of ritual and theatrical art. 'I had spent six years in St Petersburg before the war in the best days of the old Russian ballet,' writes Sir Neville Henderson, the British ambassador to Hitler's Germany, 'but for grandiose beauty I have never seen any ballet to compare with the Nuremberg rally.' One thinks of Keats—'beauty is truth, truth beauty'. Alas, the identity exists only on some ultimate, supra-mundane level. On the levels of politics and theology, beauty is perfectly compatible with nonsense and tyranny. Which is very fortunate; for if beauty were incompatible with nonsense and tyranny, there would be precious little art in the world. The masterpieces of painting, sculpture and architecture were produced as religious or political propaganda, for the greater glory of a god, a government or a priesthood. But most kings and priests have been despotic and all religions have been riddled with superstition. Genius has been the servant of tyranny and art has advertised the merits of the local cult. Time, as it passes, separates the good art from the bad metaphysics. Can we learn to make this separation, not after the event, but while it is actually taking place? That is the question.

In commercial propaganda the principle of the disproportionately fascinating symbol is clearly understood. Every propagandist has his Art Department, and attempts are constantly being made to beautify the billboards with striking posters, the advertising pages of magazines with lively drawings and photographs. There are no masterpieces; for masterpieces appeal only to a limited audience, and the commercial propagandist is out to captivate the majority. For him, the ideal is a moderate excellence. Those who like this not too good, but sufficiently striking, art may be expected to like the products with which it has been associated and for which it symbolically stands.

Another disproportionately fascinating symbol is the Singing Commercial. Singing Commercials are a recent invention; but the Singing Theological and the Singing Devotional—the hymn and the psalm—are as old as religion itself. Singing Militaries, or marching songs, are coeval with war, and Singing Patriotics, the precursors of our national anthems, were doubtless used to promote group solidarity, to emphasize the distinction between 'us' and 'them', by the wandering bands of paleolithic hunters and food gatherers. To most people music is intrinsically attractive. Moreover, melodies tend to ingrain themselves in the listener's mind. A tune will haunt the memory during the whole of a lifetime. Here, for example, is a quite uninteresting statement or value judgment. As it stands nobody will pay attention to it. But now set the words to a catchy and easily remembered tune. Immediately they become words of power. Moreover, the words will tend automatically to repeat themselves every time the melody is heard or spontaneously remembered. Orpheus has entered into an alliance with Pavlov—the power of sound with the conditioned reflex. For the commercial propagandist, as for his colleagues in the fields of politics and religion, music possesses yet another advantage. Nonsense which it would be shameful for a reasonable being to write, speak or hear spoken, can be sung or listened to by that same rational being with pleasure and even with a kind of intellectual conviction. Can we learn to separate the pleasure of singing or of listening to song from the all too human tendency to believe in the propaganda which the song is putting over? That again is the question.

Thanks to compulsory education and the rotary press, the propagandist has been able, for many years past, to convey his messages to virtually every adult in every civilized country. Today, thanks to radio and television he is in the happy position of being able to communicate even with unschooled adults and not yet literate children.

Children, as might be expected, are highly susceptible to propaganda. They are ignorant of the world and its ways, and therefore completely unsuspecting. Their critical faculties are undeveloped. The youngest of them have not yet reached the age of reason and the older ones lack the experience on which their new-found rationality can effectively work. In Europe, conscripts used to be playfully referred to as 'cannon fodder'. Their little brothers and sisters have now become radio fodder and television fodder. In my childhood we were taught to sing nursery rhymes and, in pious households, hymns. Today the little ones warble the Singing Commercials. Which is better— 'Rheingold is my beer, the dry beer', or 'Hey diddle-diddle, the cat and the fiddle'? 'Abide with me' or 'You'll wonder where the yellow went, when you brush your teeth with Pepsodent'? Who knows?

'I don't say that children should be forced to harass their parents into buying products they've seen advertised on television, but at the same time I cannot close my eyes to the fact that it's being done every day.' So writes the star of one of the many programmes beamed to a juvenile audience. 'Children', he adds, 'are living, talking records of what we tell them every day.' And in due course these living, talking records of television commercials will grow up, earn money and buy the products of industry. 'Think,' writes Mr Clyde Miller ecstatically, 'think of what it can mean to your firm in profits if you can condition a million or ten mil..on children, who will grow up into adults trained to buy your product, as soldiers are trained in advance when they hear the trigger words, Forward March!' Yes, just think of it! And at the same time remember that the dictators and the would-be dictators have been thinking about this sort of thing for years, and that millions, tens of millions, hundreds of millions of children are in process of growing up to buy the local despot's ideological product and, like well-trained soldiers, to respond with appropriate behaviour to the trigger words implanted in those young minds by the despot's propagandists.

Self-government is in inverse ratio to numbers. The larger the constituency, the less the value of any particular vote. When he is merely one of millions, the individual elector feels himself to be impotent, a negligible quantity. The candidates he has voted into office are far away, at the top of the pyramid of power. Theoretically they are the servants of the people; but in fact it is the servants who give orders and the people, far off at the base of the great pyramid, who must obey. Increasing population and advancing technology have resulted in an increase in the number and complexity of organizations, an increase in the amount of power concentrated in the hands of officials and a corresponding decrease in the amount of control exercised by electors, coupled with a decrease in the public's regard for democratic procedures. Already weakened by the vast impersonal forces at work in the modern world, democratic institutions are now being undermined from within by the politicians and their propagandists.

Human beings act in a great variety of irrational ways, but all of them seem to be capable, if given a fair chance, of making a reasonable choice in the light of available evidence. Democratic institutions can be made to work only if all concerned do their best to impart knowledge and to encourage rationality. But today, in the world's most powerful democracy, the politicians and their propagandists prefer to make nonsense of democratic procedures by appealing almost exclusively to the ignorance and irrationality of the electors. 'Both parties', we were told in 1956 by the editor of a leading business journal, 'will merchandize their candidates and issues by the same methods that business has developed to sell goods. These include scientific selection of appeals and planned repetition. . . . Radio spot announcements and ads will repeat phrases with a planned intensity. Billboards will push slogans of proven power. . . . Candidates need, in addition to rich voices and good diction, to be able to look "sincerely" at the TV camera.'

The political merchandisers appeal only to the weaknesses of voters, never to their potential strength. They make no attempt to educate the masses into becoming fit for self-government; they are content merely to manipulate and exploit them. For this purpose all the resources of psychology and the social sciences are mobilized and set to work. Carefully selected samples of the electorate are given 'interviews in depth'. These interviews in depth reveal the unconscious fears and wishes most prevalent in a given society at the time of an election. Phrases and images aimed at allying or, if necessary, enhancing these fears, at satisfying these wishes, at least symbolically, are then chosen by the experts, tried out on readers and audiences, changed or improved in the light of the information thus obtained. After which the political campaign is ready for the mass communicators. All that is now needed is money and a candidate who can be coached to look 'sincere'. Under the new dispensation, political principles and plans for specific action have come to lose most of their importance. The personality of the candidate and the way he is projected by the advertising experts are the things that really matter.

In one way or another, as vigorous he-man or kindly father, the candidate must be glamorous. He must also be an entertainer who never bores his audience. Inured to television and radio, that audience is accustomed to being distracted and does not like to be asked to concentrate or make a prolonged intellectual effort. All speeches by the entertainer-candidate must therefore be short and snappy. The great issues of the day must be dealt with in five minutes at the most—and preferably (since the audience will be eager to pass on to something a little livelier than inflation or the H-bomb) in sixty seconds flat. The nature of oratory is such that there has always been a tendency among politicians and clergymen to over-simplify complex issues. From a pulpit or a platform even the most conscientious of speakers finds it very difficult to tell the whole truth. The methods now being used to merchandise the political candidate as though he were a deodorant, positively guarantee the electorate against ever hearing the truth about anything.